IMAGES OF

THE AMERICANS FROM NORMANDY TO THE GERMAN BORDER

RARE PHOTOGRAPHS FROM WARTIME ARCHIVES

Brooke Blades

Pen & Sword
MILITARY

First published in Great Britain in 2019 by
PEN & SWORD MILITARY
An imprint of
Pen & Sword Books Ltd
47 Church Street
Barnsley
South Yorkshire
S70 2AS

ISBN 978-1-52675-672-5

Typeset by Concept, Huddersfield, West Yorkshire HD4 5JL
Printed and bound in India by Replika Press Pvt. Ltd.

Pen & Sword Books Limited incorporates the imprints of Atlas, Archaeology, Aviation, Discovery, Family History, Fiction, History, Maritime, Military, Military Classics, Politics, Select, Transport, True Crime, Air World, Frontline Publishing, Leo Cooper, Remember When, Seaforth Publishing, The Praetorian Press, Wharncliffe Local History, Wharncliffe Transport, Wharncliffe True Crime and White Owl.

For a complete list of Pen & Sword titles please contact
PEN & SWORD BOOKS LIMITED
47 Church Street, Barnsley, South Yorkshire S70 2AS, England
E-mail: enquiries@pen-and-sword.co.uk
Website: www.pen-and-sword.co.uk

Contents

Acknowledgements

My sincere appreciation must be expressed to Pen & Sword, especially Henry Wilson and Matt Jones who were willing to continue the story of the Americans and their friends in north-west Europe. I am in debt to Lori Jones and Tara Moran and the intrepid editors Barnaby Blacker and Noel Sadler.

As always, warm appreciation and affection are extended to Meg and Emma for their interest in this undertaking and patience during its preparation. My friends Jehanne Féblot-Augustins and Georges Augustins were kind to assist with identifications of Paris scenes. Graham Kelsey, specialist in many things Spanish, informed me of the participation of Amando Granell and La Nueve in the liberation of Paris.

The Irish Guards were among the most cherished of those friends to Americans in 1944 and I was delighted to learn that Henry, a former commanding officer in the regiment, met Colonel Joe Vandeleur after the war. I must thank Major Niall Hall, Adjutant, and former Colonel of the Regiment Major General Sir Sebastian John Lechmere Roberts for their assistance. Mark Hickman, who maintains the superb website Pegasus Archive, very kindly located and copied selected 1944 war diaries for the Irish Guards from the National Archives in London.

Joe French from the Commonwealth War Graves Commission generously spoke with me during a busy September weekend in Oosterbeek. Raimondo Bogaars from the Valkenswaard War Cemetery Adoption Program gave assistance with landscape interpretation for which I am grateful. The resources and staff at the US National Archives in College Park, Maryland, once again made this book possible. My gratitude is extended to Holly Reed, Kaitlyn Crain Enriquez and Sarah Lepianka in Still Pictures, Andrew Knight in Cartography and Stanley Fanaras in the General Records room.

Julie Cressman performed her usual magic in map preparation. Images of objects on display at two museums enhance the volume: Mémorial de Montormel near Chambois, France, and the Airborne Museum in Oosterbeek, Holland. One photograph derives from the collection of Library and Archives Canada (Department of National Defense fonds/a111565) in Ottawa. Three images (©IWM) were obtained from the Imperial War Museum in London.

This book is dedicated to my very good friends and former colleagues David Orr and Rick Wherley. I have learned much from them and spent many good hours in their company.

Paul Fussell in *The Boys' Crusade* recounted a story of the American soldier Austin White who carved his name in stone at Verdun in 1918 and again in 1945, saying it was the last time he wished do so. Let us hope his grandchildren and great-grandchildren and millions like them do not find it necessary to record their names at this or any other town.

Strafford, Pennsylvania
December 2018

4

Chapter One

An Army in France

After almost two months of generally slow movement through hedgerow terrain against stubborn German opposition, the Allied armies and particularly American forces in the western portion of Normandy began a dramatic breakout in late July. The face of the campaign was completely transformed by the end of August. American troops liberated most of Brittany and moved eastward along the River Loire past Orléans toward the cities of eastern France. German forces in Normandy had been encircled and while not completely destroyed were driven into pell-mell retreat. British, Canadian and American corps crossed the River Seine and one French division entered Paris. Although George Patton was referring to his own command when he considered the month as taking an army on tour, the description applied equally to all Allied forces in north-west Europe.[1]

The various corps assigned to Patton's Third Army moved rapidly once that army became operational on 1 August.

- VIII Corps moved south to Rennes and then west into the Brittany Peninsula where its units spent the remainder of the month, first driving German forces into various coastal ports and then either capturing or laying siege to those ports, such as Brest, Lorient, Saint-Malo and Saint-Nazaire. In these actions the Americans received considerable and growing support from the Forces Françaises de l'Intérieur. The ports had been important bases for German submarines preying on Allied convoys and the garrisons would mount stubborn and costly defences.
- XV Corps turned south-east to advance to Laval and beyond, with units entering Le Mans on 8 August.
- XX Corps paused to form a reserve south of Avranches following the German counter-attack near Mortain on 7 August. The counter-attack represented an intended advance to the sea at Avranches thereby cutting the American supply line to Third Army units in Brittany and to the south-east.

Mortain

The American breakout and advance through the narrow corridor at Avranches was quickly recognized for the danger it presented to the entire German position in

Normandy. A counter-offensive designed to cut off the American position was ordered by the German high command in East Prussia, which increasingly meant Hitler. Gunther von Kluge commanded Army Group B in Normandy and delayed launching the counter-attack until 7 August when most of the participating units were finally assembled. Hitler later attributed the failure of the operation to this delay and more generally to his belief that Kluge wanted it to fail. The Germans did not know, of course, that the Allies received advance indications as early as 3 August of the planned effort through decoded Enigma messages, an intelligence source known to the Allies as Ultra.[2]

Powerful armoured formations such as the 1st SS, 2nd SS and 2nd Panzer Divisions advanced westward on multiple lines towards the sea while 116th Panzer Division held a northern position. Portions of one American infantry division – the 30th – stood in the path of the advance in and around the town of Mortain approximately 18 miles inland from Avranches.

The 120th Infantry from 30th Division relieved a regiment from the 1st Division a few days before the German attack. The 2nd Battalion from the regiment was posted on high ground of Hill 317 to the east with the headquarters in the town. Early on the morning of the 7th, positions occupied by the regiment were attacked by German forces that infiltrated through the American lines in several places. The 2nd Battalion on Hill 317 was soon encircled and Mortain was overrun. The battalion commander Lieutenant Colonel Hardaway and staff hid out within the town but eventually surrendered.

A road block had been established between Mortain and L'Abbaye Blanche to the north but enemy forces wrapped around the area to encounter the 1st Battalion of the 120th in a blocking position west of Mortain. A deeper penetration by 2nd Panzer Division reached Le Mesnil-Adelée approximately 10 miles from the coast. Elements from the 119th Infantry supported by tanks from 3rd Armoured Division confronted this threat.

To the south, Germans moved into the town of Romagny and continued an advance to the south-west. Available troops from the 30th Division, primarily the 117th Infantry, engaged the forces near Romagny as others advanced to relieve Americans in Mortain. While both towns remained in enemy hands, a supply line was opened to the road block at L'Abbaye Blanche. Numerous enemy tanks were destroyed or damaged by the road block and 1st Battalion positions west of Mortain, despite receiving fire from enemy artillery and planes which were both German and Allied in origin.[3]

Enemy troops assaulted positions held by the 1st Battalion on Hill 285 early in the morning of the 8th, attacks that were driven back with American artillery support. Despite continued enemy artillery fire, the hill came under complete American control by the afternoon of the 9th, only to be partially lost again on the 10th.

By 6.30pm on the 9th, 2nd Battalion troops on Hill 317 received emissaries from the Germans who offered honourable surrender. Captain Ralph Kerley who commanded Company E replied his men would hold until they expended the last rounds and had broken their last bayonets. Enemy assaults were repelled later that evening. During the next day (10th), American planes dropped food on the hill and roughly half fell within the 2nd Battalion perimeter. During the evening medical supplies encased in former smoke shells were fired by artillery into the positions. The plasma bottles were broken but other essentials such as bandages and morphine provided comfort to some of the wounded.

A second food drop on the 11th was unsuccessful with all of the containers falling to the enemy. By that evening, however, the isolated troops knew that units from the 35th Division were nearby. On the 12th, the 320th Infantry broke through to the positions on Hill 317. Supplies were brought in and adequate care for the wounded at last began. By 1.00pm the 1/119th completed relief of positions on the hill. The commander of the 120th Infantry Colonel Birks later credited the accurate American artillery fire as a major factor enabling survival of the positions. The road block at L'Abbaye Blanche held by 2nd Battalion infantry and attached anti-tank and tank destroyer units also played a crucial role in delaying and preventing an orderly German advance.[4] Allied fighter-bomber aircraft provided devastating fire from the outset. Although none of the participating units were aware of the fact, much of the defense resulted from the Ultra information received in advance.

The Third Army Continues to Advance

On 8 August the XV Corps began to move northward to the Argentan area; units would eventually form the southern front of what became known as the Falaise Pocket. By the 14th some divisions in the Argentan vicinity began movement eastward towards the River Seine. During the same period the XX Corps moved down to the River Loire, occupying Angers on the 10th and then moved eastward to form southern defences along the river to Tours. The corps was directed on the 13th to move north-east in the direction of Chartres, which was entered on 15 August and secured the following day. XII Corps assumed responsibility for the southern line while continuing an advance to Orléans. As was the case in Brittany, these efforts received important assistance from units of the Forces Françaises de l'Intérieur (FFI) in the form of intelligence, overcoming bypassed enemy positions and guarding flanks during rapid movements.[5]

During the second half of August VIII Corps continued to isolate and attempt to overcome the various port garrisons on the Brittany Peninsula. The primary attack against the Brest garrison began on 25 August. To the east, those troops released from XV Corps gained a crossing of the Seine while others moved along the bank

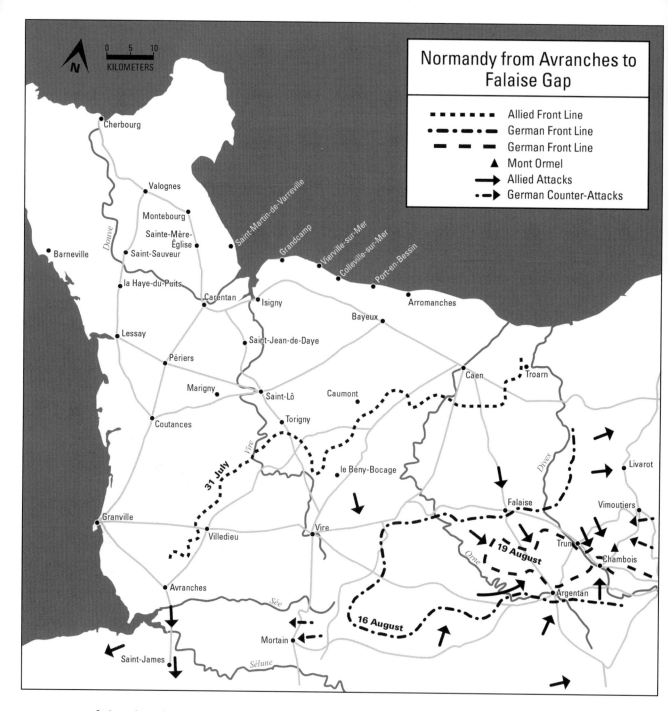

Normandy from Avranches to Falaise Gap

- ▪▪▪▪▪▪ Allied Front Line
- ▪–▪–▪– German Front Line
- ▬ ▬ ▬ German Front Line
- ▲ Mont Ormel
- → Allied Attacks
- ▪–▪▶ German Counter-Attacks

of the river in the hopes of forming a second barrier to catch Germans escaping Normandy. XX Corps continued beyond Chartres to establish other crossing points on the Seine while troops moved south of Paris to Fontainebleau and Melun.

The southern flank defence for Third Army extended along the Loire as far as Orléans by the 27th. XX Corps seized crossings of the Seine at Montereau by the

25th and continued onward. Épernay and Reims in country famous for champagne were secured.

By the end of August 90th Infantry Division followed other units into Reims and 5th Infantry reached Verdun on the River Meuse. Units from 7th Armoured Division established bridgeheads across the Meuse and 4th Armoured Division from XII Corps landed one combat command on the east bank of the Meuse in the area Saint-Mihiel and Commercy. During the last week of August the corps moved more than 70 miles eastward.[6] However, on the 29th Third Army received virtually no gasoline as supplies were allocated to offensive operations in the north.

Soldiers of the 28th Infantry in the 8th Division advance southward on 31 July as photographed by Gallo. (*NARA*)

(**Above**) Soldiers stand behind a tank destroyed during the advance into Juvigny in photograph dated 3 August. (*NARA*)

(**Opposite, above**) A smoldering Sherman tank on the outskirts of Avranches on the same day, 3 August. (*NARA*)

(**Opposite, below**) Entry to the town of Avranches on 3 August. (*NARA*)

American troops entering Avranches on 3 August. *(NARA)*

Omar Bradley with Courtney Hodges and George Patton probably in July. When Third Army became operational on 1 August, the 12th Army Group came into existence with Bradley in command. Hodges assumed control of First Army. Bradley admired both generals for different reasons. Patton was a mercurial and brilliant leader who directed spectacular advances. Hodges was considered equally intelligent but more deliberate, thoughtful and dependable. (NARA)

Wilkes recorded this view of Avranches in August. (NARA)

332085

(**Opposite, above**) A group of German prisoners captured during the breakout, in this instance photographed near Avranches on 2 August. (*NARA*)

(**Opposite, below**) An aerial view of Avranches photographed by Zwick on 2 August. (*NARA*)

(**Above**) Children and soldiers cross a temporary bridge in Avranches. DeMarco recorded the scene on 6 August. (*NARA*)

(**Opposite, above**) As Third Army troops approached the coast of Brittany they encountered a gruesome event on 7 August. The Gestapo in Morlaix previously executed fourteen men and one woman from nearby Saint-Pol-de-Léon and the local *maquis* compelled some Germans to exhume the bodies. (*NARA*)

(**Opposite, below**) A German photograph of SS panzer grenadiers resting along a hedge in Normandy. Men such as these led the counter-attack against the Avranches corridor near Mortain. (*NARA*)

(**Above**) The 12th Infantry of the 4th Division placed a 57mm anti-tank gun in Mortain on 7 August during the opening day of the attack. (*NARA*)

(**Opposite, above**) Norbie photographed troops running behind the protection offered by a hedgerow on 9 August. (*NARA*)

(**Opposite, below**) Company A 119th Infantry from the 30th Division occupied a hedgerow position near Mortain on the same day, 9 August. (*NARA*)

(**Above**) Tanks from the 2nd Armoured Division move along a hedge near Champ de Bouet, as photographed by Carolan on 10 August. (*NARA*)

(**Opposite, above**) The 120th Infantry defended this position in Le Neufbourg near Mortain with 57mm guns and bazookas that aided in stopping the armoured attack. The location was shown on 12 August. (*NARA*)

(**Opposite, below**) Medical personnel reached formerly isolated troops and established an advance aid station to treat some wounded near Mortain, as shown in this photograph by Salvas on 12 August (*NARA*)

(**Above**) Kaye recorded wrecked equipment on 13 August after the town of Mortain was recaptured. (*NARA*)

An elderly resident of Mortain returned to her home on 11 August as shown by Spangle. (*NARA*)

Chapter Two

Inferno in Normandy

As the Germans continued to attack westward near Mortain in an attempt to cut the narrow corridor of American advance through Avranches, an opportunity was offered to the Third Army troops passing through that corridor. Many streamed into Brittany and down along the Loire River. Now the divisions in XV Corps would turn east along the Loire and north towards an inter-Allied boundary established in the Argentan vicinity. First Army units pushed eastward from the Mortain vicinity.

At the same time, the combined British, Canadian and Polish forces of 21st Army Group advanced south from Caen toward the ancient town of Falaise, birthplace of William the Conqueror. If these Allied forces from the north and south could join at Argentan to form a barrier of sufficient strength, virtually all of the remaining enemy forces in Normandy would be encircled and annihilated or compelled to surrender. A spectacular victory would at last be at hand.

Troops of XV Corps advanced rapidly as they encountered little resistance in their movement from the Loire until they approached Argentan on the evening of 12 August. Patton informed Bradley that elements were near the town and asked permission to continue north to Falaise where he sarcastically proclaimed they would force the British back for 'another Dunkirk'. Reconnaissance units were nearing Falaise when ordered to halt and move back to establish a strong defensive position south of Argentan. Bradley did not wish to violate the boundary established by Montgomery. He doubted the ability of the troops present to contain the desperate remnants of roughly twenty enemy divisions and preferred a 'strong shoulder' at Argentan to a possible 'broken neck' at Falaise.[1]

Patton complained bitterly at these orders and the prospect of watching Germans escape. He argued that most of them had already moved out of the emerging pocket. Bradley disagreed and thought trapping the Germans against the River Seine might be more successful. On 14 August he allowed Patton to send the 5th Armoured and 79th Infantry Divisions east through Dreux and beyond to Mantes on the Seine. Bradley did not inform Montgomery since he thought it unlikely the latter would ask for American assistance in blocking what would soon be known as the Falaise Gap. Two days later Monty would ask for just that.

Bradley accepted responsibility for the decision to stop Patton. He did not inform Montgomery concerning the movement of two divisions eastward until 16 August when the latter called to propose an Allied junction at Chambois slightly east of the former line. As 'Monty caught his breath' when told of movement to the Seine, Bradley began to doubt the wisdom of his decision, and such doubts continued as he wrote his memoirs.[2]

A complicated tactical and command situation emerged as the strategy began to change. These complications at least partially reflected possibilities arising from mobile warfare. As a result, American forces were tearing eastward towards the Seine as other Allied troops attempted to close the gap through which German forces were desperately trying to escape.

Montgomery expected the Germans would shift their armoured units southward in response to American movement from that direction. He therefore thought the Canadians would be able to reach Falaise and move beyond to close the gap before the Americans arrived.[3] The revised junction at Chambois still made good sense since most of the German troops remained within the pocket between the Allied forces as late as 16 August.

The Germans eventually began to withdraw eastward from the Mortain area on 11 August. However, orders to renew the attack westward were issued by *Oberkommando der Wehrmacht* (OKW), on 14 August since Hitler did not accept the futility of attempts to cut off American forces near Mortain or more broadly the growing danger now confronting the entire Normandy front.

The First Canadian Army under Harry Crerar began a diversion along the road between Caen and Falaise on 12 August, with the main attack, Operation Tractable, unleashed two days later. The Germans in this sector had not participated in the Mortain counter-attack and although outnumbered resisted stoutly. This action has been criticized by the journalist Chester Wilmot and Kurt Meyer who commanded the 12th SS Panzer Division opposing the movement. Meyer was especially critical of the Canadian use of tank charges rather than emphasizing mobility and dispersal of their armour. The division was nevertheless envious of the quantity of Allied forces that seemed to stretch to the horizon on the road back to Caen.[4]

The Canadians pressed their attack and entered a devastated Falaise on 16 August, with full control of the ruined town essentially achieved the following day. The Mont Royal Fusiliers launched a final attack against roughly sixty *Hitlerjugend* in the makeshift fortress of the École Supérieure on the southern edge of town. Mortars and anti-tank guns set fire to the stone structure and drove defenders from the windows. Early on the morning of the 18th, the Fusiliers took possession of the burning building. Only four soldiers surrendered; two young soldiers left earlier with a final message for Meyer and the division. The remainder died.[5]

Kluge lost the confidence of Hitler due to failure of the Mortain counter-offensive and the fact that he had been cut off from radio communication by Allied air attacks for most of the day on 15 August. Hitler's paranoia following the July assassination attempt and hints that Kluge may have had knowledge of the plot inflamed belief that his commander in the west had attempted to contact the Allies to arrange a surrender.

On the 16th Kluge again proposed troops be withdrawn from the pocket. When a return call with Hitler's reply was not received at the promised time, Kluge began the serious attempt to evacuate. Movement resumed that evening and continued the following day. German commanders believed their retreat was aided by what they considered a lack of vigorous pursuit and concentration of Allied air attacks at the eastern end near Chambois, Trun and Vimoutiers.[6] They concluded the pocket was already closed.

Bradley ordered Patton on the 16th to use that portion of XV Corps still near Argentan to support Montgomery in closing the pocket at Chambois. These troops – 80th and 90th Infantry Divisions and the French Deuxième DB or 2nd Armoured Division – mostly covered gaps created as other units departed for the Seine.

Whatever pressure the British and Americans were exerting at the western end of the pocket, the Germans clearly understood their chances of escape rested on keeping the eastern end open. Montgomery urged Crerar to advance with all possible speed on the 17th and effect a junction with American forces in the Trun–Chambois area. As a consequence, elements of the Canadian 4th Armoured and Polish 1st Armoured divisions pushed German defenders back to the road between Trun and Vimoutiers.

Allied pressure on the pocket increased dramatically on 18 August. The nearby divisions formerly under Patton's Third Army had been transferred to Leonard Gerow's V Corps (First Army) and were launched northward in an attack ordered by Patton before the transfer. The 90th Division moved half the distance to Chambois during that day. Canadian tanks entered Trun and a small reconnaissance detachment from the South Alberta Regiment under Major David Currie with supporting Argyll and Sutherland Highlanders infantry moved further to Saint-Lambert-sur-Dives between Trun and Chambois. The Poles approached Chambois, while British forces to the west covered half the distance to Argentan. German forces remembered the night of the 18th as one of unrelenting artillery fire from all sides of the shrinking pocket.[7]

The pocket diminished by early 19 August to roughly 6 miles in depth by 7 miles in width, all of which lay within the range of some Allied gun batteries around the perimeter. During the course of the day, most German troops moved eastward across the road between Falaise and Argentan. Among them were headquarters of two armies, a panzer group, four corps and their associated troops. The once powerful armoured formations had been reduced to mere shadows. Two panzer divisions – 2nd SS and 9th SS – had escaped the pocket but were held to assist in extricating the others.

The day of 19 August was a memorable one for the Allies. Elements of the 80th Division entered Argentan and gained control of one route eastward. Troops of the 90th Division closed on Chambois from the south as a portion of the Polish 1st Armoured approached from the north. Those destined for Chambois under Major Zgorzelski included Shermans of the 24th Lancers, motorized infantry of 10th Dragoons and the 10th Mounted Rifles reconnaissance units. They entered the burning village in late afternoon to find destroyed German armour and dead or wounded soldiers. Shortly afterwards it appeared that a counter-attack might fall upon them from the south. Lieutenant Jan Karcz of the 10th Dragoons called for reinforcements and ordered his troops to open fire. The unusual reaction of the advancing soldiers – going to ground and displaying a white flag – caused the Poles to reconsider their action. The 'attackers' were in fact American infantry from the 90th Division. The forces met in the early evening and the pocket had at last been closed at Chambois.[8]

The gap, however, had not been sealed. Enemy troops continued to stream through the narrow neck south of Trun and around the Canadian cork at Saint-Lambert. The second portion of the Polish division occupied high ground north of Chambois on the road leading to Vimoutiers. This column included the 1st and 2nd Armoured Regiments commanded by Major Stefanewicz and Lieutenant Colonel Koszutski in addition to the Podolian, 8th and 9th infantry battalions with supporting anti-tank guns. Strictly speaking, they occupied the northern end of a long ridge above the village of Coudehard. General Stanisław Maczek, commander of the Polish 1st Armoured, called Mont Ormel *Maczuga* since on maps the ridge with northern and southern Hills 262 resembled a cudgel. The group of roughly eighty tanks and between 1,500 and 1,900 soldiers ascended the slopes of Mont Ormel to both initiate and in turn suffer from one of the most dramatic events in the Normandy Campaign.[9]

The northern hill offered a panoramic and commanding view of the countryside. The Polish position would soon become an isolated one, in effect an elevated island amid a sea of humanity, horses and vehicles moving eastward. For the time being, the Poles were able to concentrate their tanks and machine guns on this mass and artillery observers with them could direct the fire of distant batteries with devastating effect. One such observer, Canadian Captain Pierre Sévigny, witnessed the terrible impact of this concentrated fire. Vehicles and tanks were set ablaze and destroyed by exploding ammunition, horses held to wagons by harnesses were unable to escape, soldiers were blown into the air.[10] Artillery and tank fire was supplemented by repeated forays from Allied aircraft against which the Germans had virtually no defence.

Walter Model who replaced Kluge and Paul Hausser, commander of the German Seventh Army, still had a plan to enable as many soldiers as possible to escape. An attack from inside the pocket or *Kessel* (kettle) to widen the eastern end would be launched on the evening of 19 August. The two divisions of the II SS Panzer Corps outside the pocket would attack westward: the 9th SS towards Trun and the 2nd SS to Chambois.[11] The encircling Allied forces would thus be caught between enemy attacking from two directions. Such tactics had been successfully employed time and again on the Eastern Front to free trapped forces and had allowed some troops on the Cotentin Peninsula to escape southward.

The Poles on Mont Ormel were the unfortunate recipients of attacks from outside the pocket starting on 20 August. Troops heading for the southern end of the ridge were recalled to aid in defence as tanks and infantry from the 2nd SS struggled up the northern slope. The Germans did manage to occupy the southern end that day. They also placed troops on Hill 239 from which flanking fire could be directed into the northern end of the perimeter. The Poles had foreseen the danger but were unable to occupy that hill.

Within the perimeter, however, the Polish lines held. Enemy attacks did break through a portion of the north-eastern line in the late afternoon but were driven off. A second assault along the highway from Vimoutiers was stopped in the early evening. Sévigny could not believe his eyes. The Germans advanced in waves, at times singing *Deutschland über alles*, while the Poles held their fire until the enemy was only fifty or so paces away. When their ammunition was expended, the Poles along the line used bayonets.[12]

These attacks did not dislodge the Poles from the hill but did force a contraction of the lines. The preoccupation with defence and the smaller perimeter combined to enable a larger number of escaping German troops to move along the road below the north end of the hill, a road that led through the village of Coudehard, to Champosoult beyond the pocket.[13]

The Polish position was increasingly precarious and relief would not come from Chambois. The combined American and Polish troops were hard pressed to retain control of the town as Germans sought to dislodge them. The limited Canadian forces under Major Currie in Saint-Lambert had, like the Polish troops on Mont Ormel, held out valiantly but were too few in number to halt the enemy flow. The American divisions to the south experienced an 'artilleryman's dream' firing on the compressed columns moving near Trun.[14] Air attacks, when the weather permitted, were unrelenting.

Harried by guns on the ground and in the air, the Germans continued to struggle eastward. The troops began an aggressive push early on the 20th; an attack by the 3rd Parachute Division opened a corridor in Saint-Lambert and more generally southeast of Trun. Vehicles and guns were often lost as a result of aerial attacks or an increasing lack of fuel.[15]

Heavy rains on the night of the 20th covered the escape of thousands of German soldiers. The 277th Division with an estimated 2,500 men including 100 infantry and parachute units with around 3,000 men but no more than 600 infantry reached lines beyond the pocket at Champosoult on the morning of the 21st. The 353rd Division managed to extricate only a portion of one regiment.[16] Seventh Army commander Hausser was wounded and evacuated by an artillery unit of the 12th SS Panzers. When the general regained consciousness he threatened his benefactor with court-martial for removing him without his consent. Nothing came of the threat.[17]

The Poles on Mont Ormel thought their position might be overrun on the evening of the 20th. The exhausted troops received no supplies for days. Ammunition was almost expended and they had limited ability to care for wounded men, either their own or German. At the northern Hill 262 the commander praised their fight up to that point and said he expected they would die that night 'for Poland and civilization'.[18]

The night was relatively quiet but German attacks, again unsuccessful, resumed against the Polish perimeter on the morning of the 21st. The defenders heard the sound of more tanks to the north around midday. The Canadians were at last approaching the perimeter. The artillery observer Sévigny had been literally asleep on his feet and perhaps was still a bit groggy as he led a bayonet charge of desperate men down the slope, an anachronistic tactic in the era of airplanes and rockets. The downhill scramble was reminiscent of the charge of the 20th Maine Regiment down the slope of Little Round Top at Gettysburg. Soldiers both Polish and German were falling but nothing could stop the downward momentum. Sévigny leapt aside as a German whose rifle misfired was bayoneted. Eventually the Poles made contact with Canadian tanks and led them back up Hill 262 in triumph.[19]

A few Polish tanks also moved forward to contact the Canadian Grenadier Guards north of Mont Ormel. The scene of violence and savagery that awaited the Canadians when they entered the defensive positions was unlike anything they had seen. The Poles had been unable to evacuate their wounded while German prisoners were unguarded nearby. The roads were filled with vehicles destroyed or immobilized in the fighting. Unburied corpses covered much of the ground. The Poles on the hill were of course delighted at their relief and made long statements in Polish that were unintelligible to the Canadians who 'roared with laughter all the same'. They under-stood the international language of brothers-in-arms. The Poles held the high ground at a cost of 14 tanks and more than 650 casualties, 325 of whom died.[20]

By late in the afternoon of 21 August, the movement of German troops eastward from the pocket essentially ceased. During the previous days Allied units held prisoners from as many as twenty divisions in a single day, a clear sign of the degree of disorder during the retreat. Some abandoned the attempt to escape and simply sought refuge in the forest. Most of the units that managed to escape did so with little equipment and greatly depleted ranks. It has been estimated that 50,000 prisoners were collected and perhaps 10,000 lay dead within the confines of the pocket.[21]

The devastation of the enemy forces in the pocket defied description by most Allied observers. The French 2nd Armoured Division captured 8,800 soldiers, the American 90th Division around 13,000 in just four days. Hundreds of tanks, artillery pieces, trucks and other vehicles were destroyed or abandoned, although John Keegan was later surprised at the number that did escape. An American who visited the scene on 31 August thought it appeared as if 'an avenging angel had swept the area bent on destroying all things German'.[22] Eisenhower also toured the pocket and thought it presented images from the imagination of Dante.[23] In depicting scenes of horror with dead men and horses so closely packed that it was possible to walk great distances without stepping on the ground, he probably recalled the reaction of Ulysses Grant at Shiloh during the American Civil War.

Paul Fussell noted Eisenhower was enough of a gentleman not to mention the smell. Fussell and Florentin reminded us of the suffering of French civilians in the numerous small villages in addition to the military youth Allied and German. Fussell contended his comments were not intended as a 'pacifist' statement but the 'appalling truth' which must still be recognized at times.[24]

The failure to completely encircle the Falaise Pocket has been debated as the greatest error of the Normandy Campaign. Fingers have been pointed at a limited cast of characters. Criticisms of Montgomery's leadership in Normandy have been extended to this period. No less a supporter than Freddy de Guingan, chief of staff for 21st Army Group, recognized that the army group boundary imposed by Montgomery at Argentan was a restriction that may have prevented early closure of the gap. Both de Guingan and Wilmot believed Montgomery clearly underestimated the time it would take for the Canadians to reach Falaise.[25]

Criticism of Bradley – some self-imposed – centred on what John Keegan termed his 'Nelsonian independence' and a failure to push for closing the gap. Hastings accepted as genuine Bradley's concern that his limited forces might have been overwhelmed by the massive numbers of retreating Germans. Keegan acknowledged that Bradley's concern was probably borne out in the following days.[26]

It is impossible to ignore the role exerted by command structure within the Allied armies. The boundary issue at Argentan would not have arisen had troops on both sides of the gap been under the same – in this instance American – command.

Bradley chafed under the yoke of Montgomery's authority, which would end when Eisenhower assumed direct supervision of the land campaign on 1 September. In this context, the hands-off attitude adopted by Eisenhower remains hard to understand.

Tension and disagreement between Montgomery and Bradley/Patton emerged at various points during the fall and particularly in the winter during the bitter Ardennes Campaign. The failure to completely encircle and eliminate all of the German Seventh Army, Fifth Panzer Army and associated troops may be regarded as one of the costs of the Anglo-American alliance. There were manifold dividends in many other realms but also other costs as the war in the west progressed.

(**Above**) Flying Officer Short from RAF 181 Squadron captured this image of his Typhoon firing a rocket at escaping German vehicles near Livarot on 18 August. *(IWM)*

(**Opposite, above**) Americans advanced into the town of Argentan on the southern side of the Falaise Pocket on 19 August. Mastrosimone entered with them to record the scene. *(NARA)*

(**Opposite, below**) Troops probably from the 80th Division in Argentan on 20 August. *(NARA)*

192984

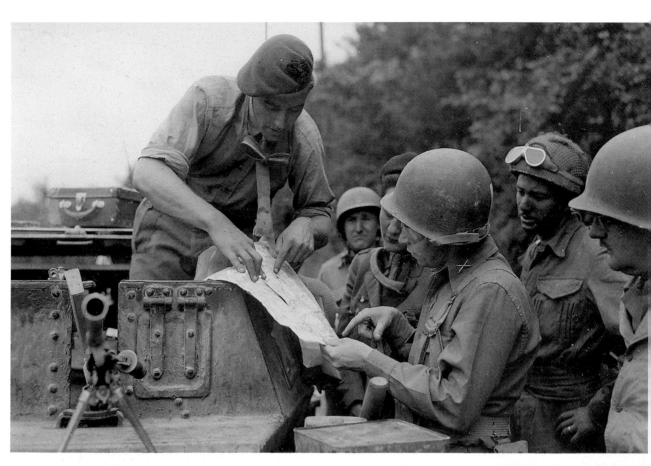

(**Opposite, above**) British Major Harold Ashby on vehicle at left met Major Harold Delp and Lieutenant Colonel Earl Diely of the American V Corps as the perimeter of the Falaise Pocket continued to shrink. Anders photographed the meeting on 19 August. (*NARA*)

(**Opposite, below**) The 90th Division entered Chambois on 19 August to meet Polish troops already in the town. An American 3-inch anti-tank gun to defend against anticipated German counter-attack was photographed that day. (*NARA*)

(**Above**) Major Leonard Dull whose battalion led the 90th Division into Chambois met with Lieutenant Vladyslaw Klaptocz of the 10th Mounted Dragoons from the 2nd Polish Armoured Division on 20 August. (*NARA*)

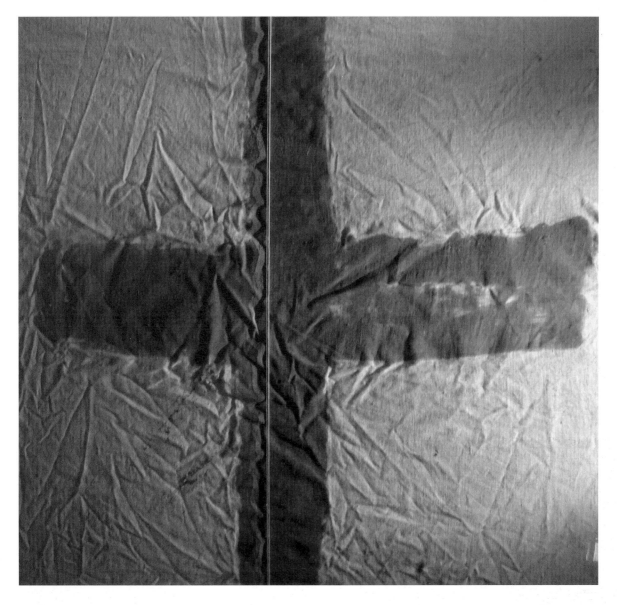

(**Opposite, above**) Wreckage of German vehicles in the town of Chambois near the bridge over the River Dives as seen on 21 August. (*NARA*)

(**Opposite, below**) The South Alberta Regiment provided reconnaissance for the 4th Canadian Armoured Division. Elements of the regiment with some tank support pushed forward to occupy a portion of the village of Saint-Lambert-sur-Dives in the middle of the Falaise Gap. Major David Currie (standing with pistol at left) from the South Albertas accepted the surrender of German troops in the village on 19 August in this photograph by Donald Grant. Other Germans struggled to cross the Dives and move past Mont Ormel to escape the Falaise Pocket. (*Mémorial de Montormel* and *Library and Archives Canada*)

(**Above**) An improvised German red cross flag recovered after 2000 from a home in Moissy near Saint-Lambert. The cross is interpreted as coloured with blood. (*Mémorial de Montormel*)

(**Opposite, above**) Makarewicz photographed a wrecked Panther tank adjacent to the 'Office de Placement Allemand' (German quarters office) in Argentan on 20 August. (*NARA*)

(**Opposite, below**) An aerial view of Argentan on 21 August. (*NARA*)

(**Above**) Debris piled in the streets of Argentan on 21 August. (*NARA*)

(**Above**) Mastrosimone saw American soldiers examining ruins near the church in Argentan on 20 August. (*NARA*)

(**Opposite, above**) Makarewicz recorded an image of members of Company I 318th Infantry outside the German quarters office in Argentan on 20 August. (*NARA*)

(**Opposite, below**) Makarewicz photographed an American unit probably from the 80th Division resting in Argentan on 20 August. (*NARA*)

(**Opposite, above**) Kitzerow saw Privates Herbert Knowles and Charles Brown, probably with the 90th Division, staring at smoke from ferocious fighting in the Falaise Gap on 20 August. (*NARA*)

(**Opposite, below**) German prisoners who survived the Falaise Gap as seen by Tomko on 20 August. (*NARA*)

(**Above**) An apparent field of surrender on which Germans dropped helmets and other equipment near Argentan on 20 August. Rough alignments of equipment evidently reflect rows in which the prisoners stood. (*NARA*)

192922-5

(**Left**) Two exhausted members of the 2nd Armoured Regiment sitting near a tank on Mont Ormel. The image was recorded by a Polish military photographer probably on 21 August after a Canadian relief column reached the defensive position held by the Poles for two days. (*IWM*)

(**Opposite**) A prisoner of war enclosure near Nonant-le-Pin in the vicinity of Argentan on 21 August contained some of the thousands of German soldiers who surrendered in the Falaise Pocket. (*NARA*)

(**Below**) Wreckage of the German army in the Falaise Gap near Chambois on 22 August. (*NARA*)

The view looking west across the Falaise Gap from the heights of Mont Ormel.

Chapter Three

'The day the war should have ended'

The liberation of Paris had not been a strategic goal of offensive operations planners following the breakout from Normandy. They argued Paris with its large population would pose a civil management challenge, while feeding and supplying the citizens would divert transport capacity desperately needed to sustain a rapid military advance. The plan called for movement around Paris to isolate the city and compel its inevitable surrender.

Such military reasoning did not consider the importance of Paris to the French resistance, the government-in-exile in London and the world at large. The city was of course a transportation centre of major importance. Far beyond that, Paris was for the French and the world a centre of culture and beauty. Its surrender in 1940 emphasized German victory in western Europe; liberation in 1944 would equally underscore the extent of Allied accomplishments since D-Day. Hitler understood as much when in the infamous 'field of ruins' order of 22–23 August he stated historical evidence proved whoever held Paris controlled France. For both the French and Germans, occupation of the city meant the liberation of France.

Several *factions résistantes* were vying for control in the city and positioning themselves for power in a post-occupation France. The movement supporting Charles de Gaulle was politically conservative, with its major strength in the countryside and the smaller towns. The more socialist and communist elements in the resistance had their greatest support within the city of Paris. Over the years de Gaulle and the French government-in-exile in Britain had directed the majority of arms drops to the countryside. As a consequence, arms and ammunition in the city were limited in the summer of 1944.

The Forces Françaises de l'Intérieur or FFI created by the government-in-exile before the invasion nominally coordinated resistance activities in the country. General Koenig, commander of the FFI in England under de Gaulle, ordered the resistance in Paris in July to halt attacks for fear of destructive reprisals. The de Gaulle organization certainly did not regard the liberation of Paris as a lower priority, but desired such liberation to occur from outside under the direction of de Gaulle.

The successful advance of Allied forces beyond Normandy toward the Seine provided a spark to the resistance in the city. The American XX Corps entered Chartres on 15 and 16 August as the XV Corps pushed forward to Mantes on the Seine west of Paris. The daily burden and humiliation of occupation after more than four years became too much for both Gaullists and leftists. Most of the railway workers went on strike and many police chose not to report to work by mid-August. On 19 August, resistance elements among the police occupied the Préfecture de Police facing Notre-Dame cathedral, in addition to *arrondissement* or district halls and police stations around the city. Various government ministries and the seat of local government, the Hôtel de Ville, were also seized. Isolated groups began firing on German patrols and vehicles at various locations within the city.[1]

The reaction of General Dietrich von Cholitz, military commander of the Greater Paris area since early August, and the German forces was limited at first but threatened to be severe. Some resistance leaders feared the outbreak of open and extensive hostilities. They knew Raoul Nordling, consul general of Sweden, maintained a relationship with Cholitz and as a result had secured the release of many political prisoners before transport to concentration camps in central and eastern Europe. The leaders now asked Nordling to suggest a cease-fire. On the evening of the 19th Cholitz informed the Swedish consul that a cease-fire would be acceptable. Earlier in the day he cancelled plans for simultaneous attacks on several known resistance command centres.

A cessation of hostilities was in the interest of both sides. The resistance would be able to avoid defeat at the hands of the Germans. The Germans could restore order in the city. Cholitz may have considered the added potential for pitting various factions of the resistance against one another.[2] In reality, Cholitz's motives were complex and at times conflicting, but he emerged as the one person who had the power to begin the destruction of Paris, but remained reluctant to do so.

Walter Model, German commander in the west, considered defence of the River Seine as a natural obstacle to the Allied advance to be more important militarily than was retention of Paris. He was, however, caught between Hitler who expected a vigorous defence, and the commander of the Greater Paris area who was increasingly determined to avoid destructive fighting in the city.

On the day following the cease-fire, Hitler through General Alfred Jodl ordered Model to defend the city, not positions to the east. The risk of destruction should not ultimately prevent such defence within the city limits. A few days later, on 22–23 August, another order decreed Paris should only be yielded to the Allies as a 'field of ruins'.

By this time the cease-fire had ended. Opposing Gaullist and communist groups differed and leftist factions carried the day in a meeting on the 21st.[3] A resistance newspaper issued the age-old order 'Aux Barricades' that led to the appearance of obstacles along and across major streets. (At times this proved difficult since boulevards had been widened by Baron Haussmann following the 1848 revolution to prevent placement of such obstacles.) Fighting resumed at intersections and near government buildings across the city. Memories of these encounters are preserved in the marble plaques affixed to buildings, such as one dedicated to Marcel Ternard, a *Gardien de la Paix* who was killed on 21 August near the Préfecture.

The situation represented a nightmare for de Gaulle. Not only did he shrink from the damage the city might sustain, but he feared control of the city might rest with his leftist opponents. He therefore pressured Eisenhower to send troops to Paris. The reality was the resistance was short of arms and munitions to sustain the fight.

De Gaulle was about to receive support from two unlikely sources. The commander of the FFI in Paris, the leftist leader Henri Tanguy known as Colonel Rol, dispatched his assistant Major Roger Gallois to Normandy to solicit arms from the Allies. During his perilous journey, Gallois became convinced to instead ask for troops to halt fighting in the city.

Cholitz also decided the only way destruction and loss of civilian life could be avoided in the city was the prompt arrival of the Allies. He contacted Nordling and suggested he go to Normandy to ask that de Gaulle be sent to the city to control the resistance. Otherwise, he felt the uprising would force his hand. Indeed, on instructions from the German high command, he had placed explosive charges on bridges and at major public monuments such as the Tour Eiffel and Napoleon's Tomb at the Hôtel des Invalides. Ultimately Nordling fell ill and his brother Rolf led a small delegation to Normandy under a written passage of safe conduct from Cholitz.

These efforts were about to coalesce with the desires of de Gaulle and the one French unit available to accomplish those desires: the Deuxième DB or 2nd Armoured Division otherwise known as the Division Leclerc. It had been decided early in the planning for Operation Overlord that Paris should be liberated by a French formation sent to Normandy for that purpose.

The armoured division commanded by General Jacques-Philippe Leclerc – a *nom de guerre* adopted to protect his family still in France – was a diverse assemblage of expatriates, adventurers from French colonies, and soldiers who had escaped from the continent and wished to continue the fight after 1940. Leclerc himself joined the forces of de Gaulle in Africa. His division landed at les Dunes de Varreville on the Cotentin coast in early August and by the middle of the month advanced along the Loire in support of Wade Haslip's American XV Corps near Argentan. When Leclerc realized on 14 August his division was among those holding the south-eastern edge of the Falaise Pocket while others were moving eastward to the Seine, he protested to Patton. In characteristically blunt fashion, Patton responded troop allocations had been based on logistical considerations, not political ones. He later recorded the conversation was difficult but they parted on friendly terms.[4]

On 21 August Eisenhower reassured de Gaulle and Koenig that the Allied command was committed to using Division Leclerc in the liberation of Paris but intended to bypass the city. De Gaulle responded he may order the French troops to enter the city on his own authority. That evening Leclerc dispatched a reconnaissance force eastward. The division had been transferred from Patton to Leonard Gerow's V Corps near Argentan. Leclerc informed his new commander of the movement the next morning. Gerow cancelled the advance and the reconnaissance force waited at Rambouillet until arrival of other divisional elements.

Undaunted, Leclerc travelled to 12th Army Group headquarters at Laval that same day. When he learned Bradley was meeting with Eisenhower at Grandcamp, he decided to await the return of the army group commander.[5] As he would soon discover, his fortunes were about to turn. Major Gallois arrived at Laval and requested immediate dispatch of a powerful force to prevent the destruction of Paris. Given the potential threat from de Gaulle and ominous news from Gallois, Eisenhower felt he had no choice but to intervene. Bradley returned to Laval and instructed Leclerc to proceed to Paris on the evening of the 22nd and avoid fighting in the city itself. Leclerc returned to his command post near Ecouché and informed the division.[6]

On the morning of the 23rd roughly 16,000 troops in several thousand vehicles began their movement to liberate the capital of France. The names assigned to units or painted on the sides of their vehicles reflected the country's long military history and diverse origins of her current army. Such units included tanks of 12e Régiment de Chasseurs d'Afrique, infantry Régiment de marche du Tchad, former sailors now in the anti-tank Régiment blindé de Fusiliers-Marins and 1er Régiment de marche des Spahis marocains that provided reconnaissance for the division.[7]

It is not difficult to imagine the excitement running through the columns that morning. For some, particularly colonial troops, Paris presented as unknown and exotic an image as for most of the Allied troops in Normandy. For others the city and routes leading to it represented their first opportunity in four years to return home.

A northern route from Sées through Rambouillet and Versailles was followed by combat commands – combined tanks, infantry and supporting troops – under Lieutenant Colonel Paul de Langlade and Colonel Dio. The southern one from Alençon through Chartres and Limours was assigned to the combat command of Colonel Pierre Billotte.[8]

As the southern march column advanced along the level plains south of Chartres, they could see the massive twin towers of the cathedral standing on the horizon. Robert Mady in the tank destroyer *Simoun* was surprised to see fields of unharvested wheat on either side of the road. The farmers were complying with instructions from the FFI in London not to harvest the crop and thereby deny the Germans access to grain.[9]

By evening of the 23rd, the northern column moved beyond Rambouillet towards Versailles and the southern column entered Limours. At this point, Leclerc changed the southern advance route and moved Dio over to assist Billotte on the south. The changes were made in part due to information Leclerc received from reconnaissance units that the southern route was less heavily defended. German outposts along these roads had been removed by the earlier advance of XX Corps, but the French armoured units would soon discover that some had been restored.[10]

Cholitz may not have been willing to undertake the destruction of Paris, but neither would he simply surrender without a show of resistance outside the city and at key points within it. German resolve was stiffened since defensive units to the south were unaware of his desire to yield control of the city to the Allies.

French movement resumed at dawn on the 24th in rainy weather that prevented use of tactical air support. Langlade's column fought for about four hours before dashing forward to Sèvres in the evening. Some units crossed the Seine into a western suburb of Paris before halting for the night. His march had been hindered not only by the Germans but by congratulations from liberated citizens along the route.

Billotte's southern column encountered stronger positions at road junctions and other locations ideal for anti-tank defence. Massy fell after two assaults but heavy fighting occurred in a concentration of strong points within the triangle between Antony, Fresnes and Croix de Berny.[11]

The ironies of fighting on one's home ground arose repeatedly during the march. Five Shermans were disabled by a single anti-tank gun at the entrance to the Fresnes prison. The crew of the tank *Marne* included Paul Landrieux who died within sight of his home on a street where he had played as a boy. For others, reunions had to be postponed. Lieutenant Henri Karcher passed through Orsay streets so mobbed with delighted citizens he did not recognize his wife and son among the crowds.[12]

Americans were mystified by what they decided was a lack of progress. Many thought the division was advancing cautiously to avoid damage to French property and perhaps indulging in celebrations. Bradley expressed concern that Cholitz might change his mind if he received reinforcements. While recognizing the outpouring of emotions en route, Bradley stated he could not allow the French to 'dance' into the city and ordered the American 4th Infantry Division to join the advance.[13] When the Division Leclerc reported its losses at the end of August – most of which had been sustained during the advance – the strength of the opposition appeared more significant than had been imagined. These losses included 317 soldiers, 71 of whom were killed, and 152 vehicles including 35 tanks.

Leclerc had been instructed to continue movement during the evening of the 24th and he was also aware the 4th Division would join the hunt shortly. He therefore sent Captain Raymond Dronne with the Tchad infantry and three tanks from the Régiment de Chars de Combat – *Champaubert, Montmirail* and *Romilly* – to bypass any opposition and enter the city. Avoiding larger roads likely to be defended, Dronne's small force entered at the Porte d'Italie, passed stunned then ecstatic crowds at the Place d'Italie and drove through the south-eastern quarter towards the Seine. They crossed the river on the Pont d'Austerlitz after ignoring a burst of machine gun fire, moved along the north bank of the Seine, and halted at the Hôtel de Ville shortly after 9.00pm. The first French troops arrived in Paris more than four years after Germans had marched into the city. Dronne informed the overjoyed if somewhat unprepared hosts that the balance of Division Leclerc would arrive the following day.[14] Dronne's infantry company – the 9th or 'La Nueve' – consisted mostly of Spanish Republican veterans effectively led by the Valencian Amando Granell.[15] The Republicans gained a measure of revenge over the fascists that evening in Paris.

Elements of the 12th Infantry of the 4th Division began their march along the Seine early on the morning of the 25th. The regiment had landed at Utah Beach on D-Day and had sustained more than 4,000 casualties in Normandy. Earlier that month, they suffered 1,000 dead and wounded near Mortain. Most of the foot soldiers that had landed on 6 June were no longer with the regiment to witness the liberation.[16]

The 12th Infantry advanced along the west side of the Seine but German gun-fire from the opposite bank forced troops inland away from the river along an undefended route. Before noon, advance elements arrived in front of Notre-Dame cathedral. As one American soldier commented, it was 'the day the war should have ended'.

The various elements of Division Leclerc entered the city from three directions. Langlade moved from the western suburbs to the Arc de Triomphe. Billotte's troops from the south crossed the Seine over the Île de la Cité to the Place du Châtelet. These two groups would later meet along the Champs-Élysées. A column under Dio moved into the south-western district of the city towards the École Militaire and the Palais Bourbon, home of the Chamber of Deputies.

These troop columns generated outpourings of joy that had waited four years to be expressed. The *tricolore* flag of France, either hidden during the occupation or recently sewn by hand, flew throughout the city. Dresses and costumes put aside for this day were worn by *parisiennes* young and old. Food, wine and flowers were pressed into the hands of French and American soldiers.

Others awaited the arrival of the Division Leclerc with dread and resolution. The soldiers of Cholitz continued to defend various strongpoints across the city. Fighting of surprising intensity occurred at locations on the Left Bank of the Seine. Opposition was encountered at the École Militaire and the Palais Bourbon, as well as along the Quai d'Orsay and nearby Hôtel des Invalides. Germans also defended the Palais du Luxembourg – seat of the French Senate in happier times – at the head of some of the largest and loveliest gardens in Paris.

Ironies of fighting on familiar ground continued on this day of liberation. Several soldiers contacted family members by telephone during the march or upon entering the city only to be killed before reunions could occur. The tank destroyer *Simoon* arrived at the Étoile surrounding the Arc de Triomphe amid an impromptu celebration when a shell fired by a Panther tank in the Place de la Concorde whistled through the Arc. Robert Mady in *Simoun* recalled the exact distance down the Champs-Élysées, set the gun range to 1,800 metres and disabled the tank with one shot.[17]

The French learned that Cholitz in the Hôtel Meurice would surrender following a show of resistance. Tchad infantry and Régiment de Chars de Combat tanks headed west in the early afternoon past the Louvre and down the Rue de Rivoli to provide the Germans with a last stand in Paris. Events bizarre, tragic and humorous unfolded along what John Keegan termed a 'battlefield de luxe' due to the exclusive shops and cafés situated under the early-nineteenth-century colonnade opposite the Tuileries Gardens.[18]

Armoured vehicles entered the Place de la Concorde, considered by many the most beautiful square in the world. The gunner of tank destroyer *Filibuster* opened fire on the elegant façade of the eighteenth-century palace housing the Hôtel Crillon. It was said that he had been warned to look out for 'fifth columnist' collaborators and accordingly destroyed the 'fifth column' from the south-east corner with a well-placed shot.[19]

The Sherman tank *Douaumont* entered the Place de la Concorde and spied the Panther immobilized by Mady and *Simoun*. Realizing the Panther's 75mm gun was still operable, the French tank crew fired the wrong ammunition – high-explosive rather than armour-piercing – with little effect. Sergeant Michel Bizen, a Breton on his first visit to Paris, ordered the driver to ram the Panther. He then leapt down with a grenade to complete the destruction. As *Douaumont* backed away, Bizen stood in the turret and was killed by German fire from the roof of a building on the north side of the square.

The advance of the Tchad infantry and supporting tanks was punctuated by brief but violent bursts of fire. One of their infantry captains was cut down by a machine gun. Three Germans were blown apart in front of the golden statue of Jeanne d'Arc in the Place des Pyramides. Several Shermans were disabled by enemy fire or grenades thrown into open hatches.

Shelter provided by broad columns of the arched passage along the Rue de Rivoli aided the infantry advance to the Meurice. They entered under cover of a burst of gunfire and grenades. Lieutenant Henri Karcher now demanded to be shown to the office of the German commander.

Cholitz and his staff were waiting when the grimy Karcher entered. The latter, quite nervous, asked the German commander if he spoke German. Cholitz responded,

'Probably better than you'. Karcher then asked for and received the surrender of the commander of the Greater Paris area to the army of General de Gaulle.[20]

The former commander was led through angry crowds and driven to the Préfecture de Police where Leclerc was seated at a luncheon. Cholitz signed a formal act of capitulation. Leclerc signed for the Provisional Government of France. Colonel Rol arrived and insisted on inclusion as a signatory on behalf of the FFI in Paris. Leclerc then bundled Cholitz into a vehicle for a trip to the French division headquarters at the Gare Montparnasse. Troops were then dispatched throughout Paris to inform Allied and German forces that this portion of the war had ended.

Stories of that first night of liberation in the City of Light are legendary and include a slightly fictionalized account by Ernest Hemingway set in the Hôtel Ritz.[21] The troops of the Division Leclerc and the 4th Division would move beyond the city limits over the next few days. The Americans assembled in the Bois de Vincennes and resumed their advance on the 27th. Soldiers in the 12th Infantry saw Notre-Dame and the Tour Eiffel. Many carried memories of gratitude and tender encounters that would last a lifetime. Some formed lifelong friendships or established romances leading to marriage. Others spent their last day of life in the city. Soon the division would be far to the north-east of Paris.

General Jacques-Philippe Leclerc landing at Les Dunes de Varreville on the Cotentin coast, 2 August, as photographed by Kaufman. (NARA)

One of the Sherman tanks from Division Leclerc, also known as the Deuxième DB, rolls off an LST (landing ship tank) onto French sand at Les Dunes de Varreville on 1 August. (*NARA*)

(**Opposite, above**) Elements of the Division Leclerc assembled inland on the Cotentin possibly on 1 August. The division used American vehicles, weapons and uniforms and followed American principles of combat commands. The names assigned to units or painted on vehicles reflected French heritage and geography. (*NARA*)

(**Above**) The magnificent Notre-Dame cathedral in Chartres was rebuilt in a remarkably short time following a devastating fire in 1194. This view was recorded by Sullivan on 18 August 1944. George Patton entered the town a few days earlier with XX Corps troops. He first visited in the 1920s and returned to see the cathedral, commenting the interior architecture could be appreciated since removal of stained glass windows allowed more light inside. (*NARA*)

(**Opposite, below**) An African American artillery unit serving with Third Army loading a shell labelled 'From Harlem to Hitler' in the vicinity of Mantes-Gassicourt on the Seine on 20 August. (*NARA*)

(**Above**) Dwight Eisenhower met with Charles de Gaulle in Normandy on 21 August. Matters under discussion bore directly on the possible threats posed by the Germans to Paris and of the need for Allied – in this case French – troops to enter the city. (*NARA*)

(**Opposite, above**) American troops probably from XX Corps look across the open plains to Chartres on 21 August as photographed by Sullivan. The distinctive twin towers of the cathedral were plainly visible. Hay or straw has been cut and stacked in piles in the fields, but Robert Mady would note local farmers had not harvested wheat when the Division Leclerc passed through on 23 August. (*NARA*)

(**Opposite, below**) The Forces Françaises de l'Intérieur (FFI), or the resistance, began an uprising in Paris resulting in occupation of buildings, scattered ambushes and creation of barricades across streets and on bridges. One such barricade stood on the northern end of the Pont Neuf that despite its name was the oldest bridge over the Seine. This photograph dated 26 August illustrates the mixed blend of police and resistance forces in the city. Weaponry was also mixed and included a captured German machine gun. (*NARA*)

193233

(**Opposite, above**) Another barricade blocked a street junction at the Hôtel Raphael near the Étoile that surrounded the Arc de Triomphe. This 26 August photograph shows soldiers probably from the Division Leclerc with a dead German lying in the foreground. (*NARA*)

(**Opposite, below**) The French division approached the southern outskirts of Paris on 24 August when German defences were encountered in Antony. The photographer Gedicke accompanied the armoured column on the march. (*NARA*)

(**Above**) General Leclerc observed the advance of his division into Paris on 25 August. Images of Leclerc usually depict a stoic soldier, but the smile of the nearby aide reflected a day enshrined in legend. (*NARA*)

(**Opposite, above**) Small battles erupted across the city on the 25th as the Germans waged final defensive stands. This view facing north shows from left to right the church spires or domes of Saint-Augustin, Sacré-Coeur on the high ground of Montmartre and Sainte-Clotilde. Smoke was rising from armed encounters near police stations in the northern districts of the city. (*NARA*)

(**Opposite, below**) Another view across the rooftops facing south-west towards the Tour Eiffel revealed smoke columns rising from several battles between defenders and the Division Leclerc. The dome of the Invalides is visible at the left margin. (*NARA*)

(**Above**) Kitzerow recorded this image on the 25th of 4th Division soldiers in the city. (*NARA*)

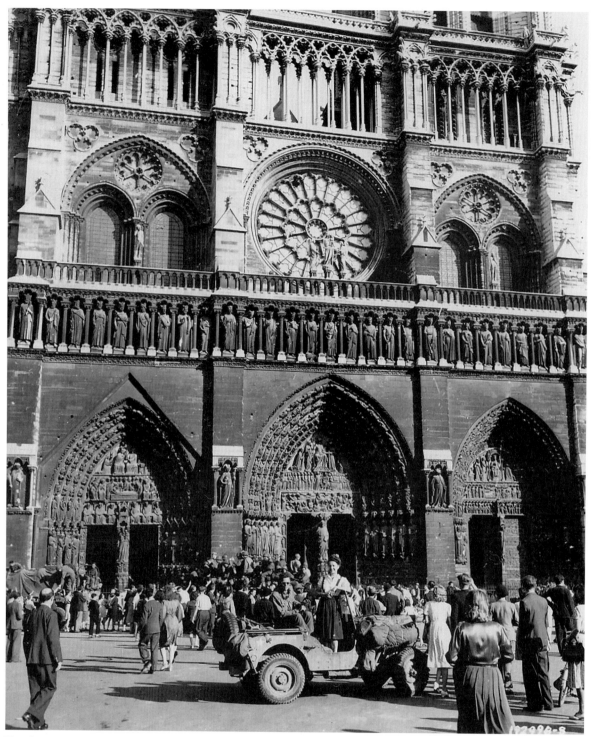

The façade of Notre-Dame cathedral, one destination of the 4th Division. (*NARA*)

The famous (or for some wives or girlfriends in America infamous) image of the 'kiss' in France. This one was bestowed on 4th Division Sergeant Kenneth Averill from Michigan by a *parisienne* and was recorded by Verna on the day following the liberation. (*NARA*)

(**Opposite, above**) The Rue de Rivoli on the day following liberation. An abandoned tank with a sloping deck suggesting a Sherman attracted much attention. The tank was knocked out during the advance along the street to the Hôtel Meurice. (*NARA*)

(**Opposite, below**) The Arc de Triomphe on the 26th. A shell fired from a Panther tank passed through the arch near the *tricolore* flag on the previous day. (*NARA*)

(**Above**) Verna recorded crowds around tanks in the Place de la Concorde on the 26th. The façade of the Hôtel Crillon with the missing 'fifth' column is visible. (*NARA*)

(**Above**) German prisoners in the lobby or ballroom of the Hôtel Majestic in Paris on the 25th. (*NARA*)

(**Opposite, above**) German officers grouped in the Majestic on the 26th. (*NARA*)

(**Opposite, below**) A firing range for the execution of French prisoners in the basement of the Ministry of Aviation near the Tour Eiffel (Collins and Lapierre, *Is Paris Burning?*) was shown in this 31 August photograph. (*NARA*)

193010-S

(**Right**) Parisians gather at the Place du Président Mithouard on the 25th, 'the day the war should have ended'. (*NARA*)

(**Opposite**) Notre-Dame façade with Division Leclerc vehicles arranged in front on the 26th. (*NARA*)

(**Below**) A view of the Place de la Concorde and the Hôtel Crillon on the day following liberation. (*NARA*)

193345

193373

(**Opposite, above**) A massive crowd gathered around the Arc de Triomphe on the 26th. (*NARA*)

(**Opposite, Below**) A group of *parisiennes* in traditional and dress costumes became impromptu participants in the parade on the Champs-Élysées. (*NARA*)

(**Above**) General de Gaulle marched down the Champs-Élysées on the 26th accompanied by Generals Koenig at right and Leclerc in the centre rear. (*NARA*)

(**Left**) A young woman with a stylish head scarf or hat symbolized the end of the occupation on the 27th. (*NARA*)

(**Below**) Another symbolic treatment on the same day, in this case for women accused of collaboration: clothes torn, heads shaven and foreheads painted with swastikas. (*NARA*)

(**Opposite**) A parade of American forces was requested after the liberation. The 28th Division arrived in the Bois de Boulogne to wash themselves and their vehicles on 28 August and paraded down the Champs-Élysées the following day. (*NARA*)

93200-S

Kitzerow recorded an image of a fellow photographer lying between marching columns during the parade. Such an action would be even more dangerous today given traffic in the city. (NARA)

A classic image of the liberation: American soldiers from the 28th Division parade down the Champs-Élysées in Paris. The division marched through the city to waiting trucks that transported them to the battle front near the city the same day, 29 August. (NARA)

Chapter Four

To the Border

The German collapse in Normandy and failure to use the Seine or Marne as a defensive line meant Allied armies would now tear across France. As celebrations erupted in Paris, much of the American First Army drove past the French capital for the eastern and northern borders. Their units entered Namur on the River Meuse south-east of Brussels on 4 September and pushed on into Luxembourg and eastern Belgium. Both countries were liberated by the middle of September.

British and Canadian forces progressed to the Seine as Paris was liberated and soon began spectacular advances through battlegrounds of the First World War in northern France and into southern Belgium. After an all-night march preceded by more than a day of movement, tanks and troop carriers of the British 11th Armoured Division with XXX Corps entered Amiens along the River Somme on the morning of 31 August. The Guards Armoured Division led a march that carried XXX Corps into Brussels on 3 September, where joyous celebrations were the order of the day. Not to be outdone, the 11th Armoured Division seized Antwerp on 4 September.[1] At long last, the Allies had a functional port close to their front lines where the harbour facilities remained intact. The surprised Germans did not have enough time to disable the port.

However, the Allies failed to realize that possession of Antwerp was meaningless unless they also controlled the shorelines along the roughly 60 miles of the Schelde (or Scheldt) estuary leading from the North Sea to the port. The naval chief on Eisenhower's staff, Admiral Bertram Ramsey, emphasized this concern and Ultra intelligence revealed the importance Hitler placed upon holding the shorelines and islands along the estuary. Nevertheless, Allied attention focused eastward to the Rhine and Ruhr industrial district. In addition, Ultra data revealed the Germans were ferrying large numbers of troops across the estuary and past Antwerp into Holland. These troops among others would shortly stiffen the German defence of the corridor north from Eindhoven.

The American Third Army was moving well to the east of Paris. XX Corps captured towns on the Seine on the 25th, the 5th Infantry Division moved northward and captured Épernay and Reims on successive days, 28 and 29 August. Seventh Armoured Division passed through Verdun on the Meuse and during the first week

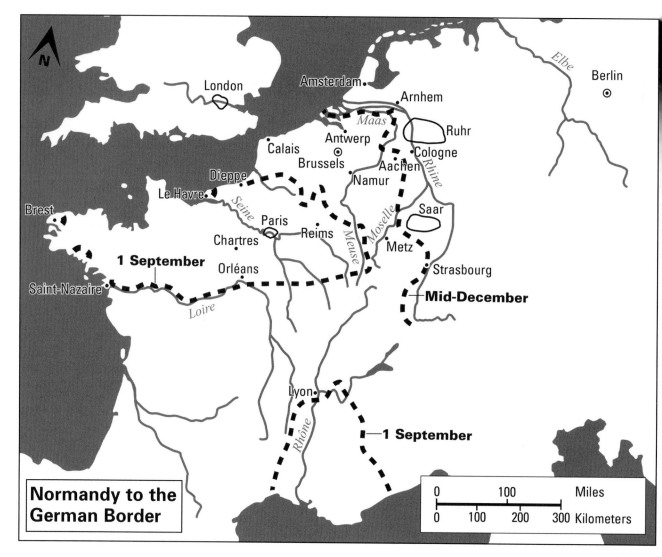

Normandy to the German Border

of September advanced towards Metz on the River Moselle. An effort to capture Metz began as early as 17 September.

Combat Command A, 4th Armoured Division, seized crossings over the Moselle at Dieulouard south of Metz and Pont-à-Mousson on 13 September and continued eastward. Combat Command B from the division crossed the Moselle further south beyond Nancy and pushed eastward in an effort to meet Combat Command A moving from the north to form an enlarged bridgehead. The 35th Infantry Division crossed the river even earlier on the 10th south of Nancy while the 80th moved across to the north. The city fell to the Third Army on 15 September.[2]

Captured soldiers began to fill Allied prisoner of war enclosures from Normandy across France and into Belgium. Rations including those served to prisoners of war became an issue. The Geneva Convention stipulated that prisoners would be served food in quantities and quality equal to those available to soldiers in base camps. As prisoners were increasingly retained on the continent due to shortages of shipping and the need for prisoner labour, supplies for them were subject to the same limitations experienced by the Allied armies. In addition, a degree of public complaint arose in America when reports of malnutrition among Allied prisoners in Germany emerged. As a result, a postwar Quartermaster report stated the spirit if not always the letter of the Convention was followed.[3]

Bill Mauldin adopted a different interpretation with regards to rations. He thought the German sausage and marmalade were good. Since he felt most of the ingredients probably derived from France, he concluded that after Normandy the quality would decrease. When the enemy supply chain was not disrupted by air attacks, it seemed to be effective and emphasized transport of the best foods to the front lines. Mauldin contended German prisoners complained about their rations in captivity and refused to believe American soldiers were served the monotonous canned C rations.[4]

Criticism of the slow Allied progress during June and July in Normandy seemed a distant concern. However, success, particularly when rapid, brought its own challenges. Since late July the issue of strategy in the event of a sudden German collapse became increasingly urgent. The American forces divided into separate armies under the command of Omar Bradley and 12th Army Group. Movement into Brittany continued, but the importance of the province and its ports as specified in the SHAEF operational plan steadily decreased with spectacular advances to the east and north.

As the Allies broke free of the Norman hedgerows and drove remnants of the Reich's western armies across France, strategic differences became more focused and intense, even bitter. The strategic debate has come down in history in a simplified fashion as the contrast between the narrow front or single thrust advocated by Montgomery and the equally firm belief held by Eisenhower that continued movement along the broad front from the North Sea to the Alps was necessary. The debate continued from late summer 1944 into the winter of 1945 and was never resolved during the war in Europe. The fates of thousands of soldiers and millions of civilians would hinge on the decision.

Eisenhower assumed direct control of land operations beginning 1 September but Montgomery continued to promote a 'full-blooded' thrust along the northern portion of the front. The purpose was to secure a crossing of the Rhine and encircle the essential German industrial Ruhr region using British forces in the north and the American First Army from the south. Combined armies of twenty or more divisions subduing the Ruhr would, he argued, render German capacity to continue the war difficult if not impossible. Beyond that, however, he was confident a collection of twenty to forty divisions could make an unstoppable march to Berlin. To accomplish this, Montgomery expected to control his own 21st Army Group and the US First Army, thereby relegating Patton and Third Army to maintaining a strong defensive position from Reims south to the Orléans Gap between the Rivers Seine and Loire.[5]

Eisenhower envisioned offensives in Normandy along broader fronts akin to those practised by the Russians in the east. He was no doubt impressed by the success of Operation Bagration launched in late June that tore a wide opening in the German lines, regaining much of Belorussia into Poland by late July in the process. Twenty-eight German divisions were eradicated with the loss of 300,000 killed or captured in a campaign known as the Destruction of Army Group Centre.[6]

Since Eisenhower anticipated exerting direct control of the ground forces, he believed a broad front advance was the proper strategy to pursue in the west. The American Seventh Army and French First Army landed on the Riviera in mid-August and advanced up the Rhône Valley with the ultimate goal in Eisenhower's plan of meeting Patton's forces in eastern France. He hoped to seize both the Ruhr and Saar regions and if possible to cross the Rhine before the onset of winter. For reasons both military and political, he was loath to halt the advance of Third Army that had achieved such dramatic results since becoming operational on 1 August. Despite potential difficulties, Ike remained convinced Patton understood the possibilities of mobile warfare as well or better than any Allied commander and advocated on his behalf with George Marshall and Bradley.

Nevertheless, Eisenhower did agree to give priority of sorts to the 21st Army Group (British/Canadian armies) and the American First Army in late August. On 29 August Patton learned that an expected 140,000 gallons of gasoline were not delivered. He insisted his commanders establish crossings over the Meuse even if such movement required draining fuel from some tanks and vehicles to fill others. He discovered supply planes were diverted to assist in feeding the citizens of Paris and support the major effort undertaken by First Army and the British to the north. Patton later considered 29 August to be a critical day during the war and believed the decision to deprive his army of support a monumental mistake.[7]

Perspectives

The importance of an acrimonious meeting at an airfield in Brussels on 10 September between Montgomery and Eisenhower over strategy must be considered. Ike later stated he thought Montgomery was 'nuts' for proposing a narrow northern advance requiring constant diversion of divisions to protect an exposed southern flank.[8] During the meeting Monty presented the plan for Market Garden. Eisenhower, under considerable pressure to make more imaginative use of the new Allied airborne army, approved the plan to invade Holland. However, Ike never viewed the operation as the sole Allied thrust but hoped for a crossing of the Neder Rijn at Arnhem that could be exploited for further offensives in the north.

Montgomery clearly desired a more important role in the decisive climax of the war while under pressure to do something about German rocket attacks launched from the North Sea and Baltic coasts. Nevertheless, this desire and the general spirit of optimism should have been tempered by intelligence from Ultra and the Dutch resistance that German forces were increasing and included battered but still first line SS panzer divisions in the area of the proposed Market Garden action. In addition, Germans were ferrying troops across the Schelde from their Fifteenth Army that had been bypassed in northern France and coastal Belgium, actions also indicated by Ultra.[9]

The overwhelming concern was – or should have been – one of supply: seizing Antwerp without clearing the long estuary of the Schelde to the North Sea was meaningless. British forces had not grabbed bridges across the Albert canal until it was too late to do so, nor had they advanced the additional 15 miles to cut off the narrow isthmus connecting the South Beveland peninsula to the mainland. Many German soldiers ferried north across the Schelde escaped through South Beveland. Horrocks would later acknowledge Napoleon would have realized these things but 'Horrocks did not'. Indeed, he would state the day Antwerp fell – 4 September – would later be recognized as the one on which the Battle of Arnhem was lost.[10]

Liddell Hart provided an interesting perspective based in part on German opinions gleaned from postwar interviews. He concluded conditions favoured a single thrust for a brief period in late August, but the location seemed to matter less than the effort be a strong one conducted without pause. He argued that resumption of supplies to Patton around 5 September was not really the detrimental element derided by most British analysts and directed attention to factors as major as transport diverted to support a cancelled airborne operation near Tournai (Bradley correctly predicted his infantry would arrive before the operation could come off) and as seemingly minor as defective pistons that rendered more than one thousand British lorries unusable. He felt the best chance for an Allied advance resulting in a complete German collapse lay with Third Army in late August and cited Patton's belief that military success depended upon the rapid modification of strategic plans to fit changing conditions.[11]

Horrocks believed each commander was correct from his own perspective and that Eisenhower made the proper decision from his broader strategic concerns. He did contend that if resources held back for Market Garden, particularly transport aircraft, had been available in early September, the ground advance may have secured a crossing of the Rhine and possibly ended the war in 1944.[12]

Freddy de Guingand, Montgomery's chief of staff, described the debate as the only issue on which he disagreed with his former superior. Had the effort been undertaken as Monty desired, Freddy thought a crossing of the Rhine may have been achieved by winter but nothing more.[13]

Generals Bradley and Patton on 31 August en route to visit troops in Brittany. By this time some Third Army divisions besieged ports in that province while others moved eastward across France at a rapid pace. Supply shortages particularly of gasoline began to slow movement to the east. (NARA)

American air commanders Spaatz, Quesada, Conner and Eaker stand outside Eisenhower's headquarters in Normandy when photographed by Moore on 4 September. General Quesada embraced the new role of tactical support for infantry and armoured forces that paid such dividends in Normandy and later in the campaign in north-west Europe. (NARA)

Eisenhower visited Montgomery at the latter's tactical headquarters during Operation Cobra on 26 July. One of Monty's pair of terriers, Hitler and Rommel, also attended the conference. By early September strong disagreements erupted on strategy following the German collapse in Normandy. *(NARA)*

(**Above**) The 8th Infantry from the 4th Division advanced under fire into Libin, Belgium. Gedrick photographed the scene on 7 September. (*NARA*)

(**Opposite, above**) American soldiers probably from the same regiment sought shelter near a jeep while under fire in Libin on the same day. (*NARA*)

(**Opposite, Below**) Private Elbert Hall from California landed with the 4th Division and was wounded in Normandy. He was treated for a second wound suffered near Libin on 7 September. (*NARA*)

(**Opposite, above**) Two 8th Infantry soldiers sought a warm and reasonably comfortable sleep in a haystack near Libin on the evening of 7 September. (*NARA*)

(**Opposite, below**) Soldiers from Company I in 60th Infantry of the 9th Division advance slowly into a town in eastern Belgium, using a Sherman tank for cover. (*NARA*)

(**Above**) This photograph has been published as 'assault on Arnhem' but the date of 10 September if accurate undermines that identification. The image evidently shows a bursting artillery or mortar shell among infantry, possibly with the XIX Corps advancing near Maastricht towards the German border. (*NARA*)

Combat Command A of the 4th Armoured Division crossed the River Moselle at Dieulouard south of Metz and Pont-à-Mousson in eastern France on 13 September. Mastrosimone recorded a sign being prepared by the FFI in Dieulouard. The message was simple: no German prisoners were to be taken due to their behaviour in the vicinity. (*NARA*)

As had been the case in France, those accused of association with German soldiers were punished in Belgium. Women whose hair had been cut off were further humiliated by swastikas painted on their foreheads. Barth recorded this scene in Lanaken near Liège on 15 September. (*NARA*)

Chapter Five

'When in doubt, lash out'

During a meeting at the headquarters of the First Allied Airborne Army on Sunday evening, 10 September, James Gavin learned of Operation Market Garden. The briefing, led by General Frederick 'Boy' Browning, described plans for the '82nd to seize the bridges at Grave and Nijmegen and high ground between Nijmegen and Groesbeek' in Holland. Other airborne divisions would participate: the 101st dropping to the south near Eindhoven and the 1st British Airborne, supported by the Polish Parachute Brigade, landing to the north to capture a bridge across the Neder Rijn at Arnhem. The purpose was to secure a corridor over which the British XXX Corps could advance from the Belgian border across the Rhine. The planned date for commencing the operation floated around but after a few days settled on Sunday, 17 September. Gavin concluded his entry: 'It looks very rough. If I get through this one I will be very lucky. It will, I am afraid, do the airborne cause a lot of harm.'[1]

The operation combined parachute and glider troops in the Market phase, with British armoured and infantry forces in the Garden portion. The airborne forces would land during daylight and secure as many bridges along the corridor as possible on the first afternoon or evening. Military planners realized these forces would not be able to withstand attacks once enemy ground forces gathered en masse. Given the speed of the advance following the German collapse in Normandy, it was thought XXX Corps would move up the corridor to Arnhem in two or three days. Local enemy forces were expected to be relatively few in number and disorganized. Such opposition could be dealt with until the armour and infantry arrived.

* * *

General Brian Horrocks, commander of XXX Corps, briefed brigadiers and battalion colonels in a theatre near the Belgian-Dutch border on 16 September. His forces consisted of the 43rd and 50th Infantry Divisions, the Guards Armoured Division and the 8th Armoured Brigade. He explained in great detail the Garden portion and preparations organized during the past week. He announced that following an extensive artillery pounding of the enemy lines on the early afternoon of 17 September, the Irish Guards group would lead the advance into Holland. The landscape was

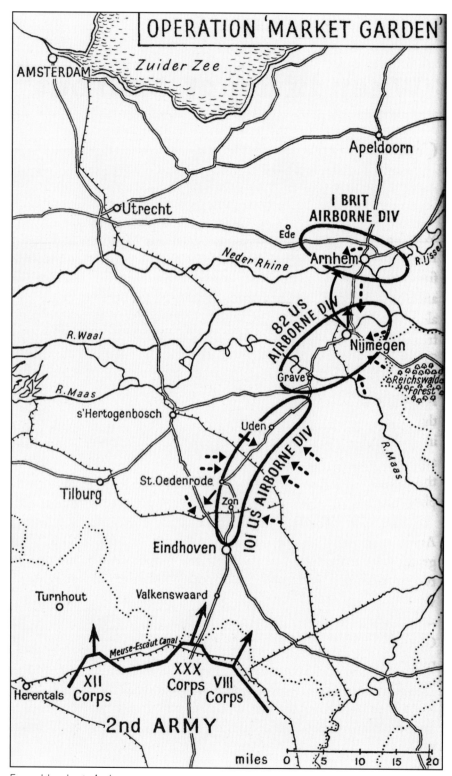

From Urquhart, *Arnhem*.

described as low lying ground with woods and swamps. The troop columns would advance and be supplied along a single road extending northward. He emphasized speed was essential and if at all possible the corps should reach and cross the Neder Rijn into Arnhem in two days.[2]

The next day Horrocks watched from a factory roof as Lieutenant Colonel Joe Vandeleur assembled the Irish Guards armoured and infantry column to await the opening barrage. By noon confirmation messages indicated that waves of fighter planes and transport aircraft carrying the 101st Airborne were on their way. Artillery barrages including medium and heavy gun fire on the road to Valkenswaard began around 2.00pm. Roughly thirty minutes later shells from 240 field guns landed 1,000 yards north of the start line and 'walked forward' at 200 yards per minute towards the apparent locations of German positions. Lieutenant Keith Heathcote led the tanks of 3rd Squadron, 2nd Battalion Irish Guards, across the start line at 2.30pm. Despite great clouds of dust raised, leading tanks followed about 300 yards behind the exploding shells.[3]

All seemed to go well for ten minutes until Heathcote looked back to see the rear portion of his squadron and front part of 1st Squadron already in flames or being struck by anti-tank rockets and gunfire. The German front line had been damaged but not eliminated and a battle ensued just over the border into Holland. Infantry from the Irish Guards 3rd Battalion deployed in the fields and began to fire on the German positions. RAF liaison officers called down more than 200 rocket sorties by Typhoons on those positions during the ensuing hour. When Germans were finally subdued, it was discovered they were members of the 6th Parachute Regiment supported by self-propelled guns. The Irish Guards lost nine tanks, fifteen killed and more than twenty wounded. Among those killed was Squadron Sergeant Major W. Parkes, who previously survived the loss of a tank in Normandy.

The column reassembled and advanced as far as Valkenswaard on the River Dommel where it halted for the night. They were cheered by the news the 82nd Airborne had seized the Grave bridge over the River Maas (Meuse) and at least one crossing of the Maas–Waal canal. The 101st captured bridges between Eindhoven and Grave but not the Son bridge over the Wilhelmina canal. No definite word revealed events at the northern end of the corridor, specifically the River Waal bridges in Nijmegen and the Neder Rijn bridge into Arnhem. Intelligence officers discovered opposing forces contained numerous units 'which had no right to be there'.[4] The Irish Guards entered Eindhoven the following day but would be unable to cross the Wilhelmina canal until early morning on the 19th when the Grenadier Guards led the advance of Guards Armoured Division northward.[5]

*　*　*

The regiments of the 101st Airborne experienced nearly perfect landings on their jump zones allowing rapid assembly and deployment to various objectives. Some gliders had difficult landings and occupants were injured. The executive officer of the 506th Parachute Infantry found two men in the field 'cut up' by following planes after they jumped. The regiment was responsible for securing the Wilhelmina canal bridge in Son but by evening it was reported damaged or destroyed.[6]

Another bridge spanned the canal between Eindhoven and Best to the north-west and initially a single company from the 502nd Parachute Infantry had been detailed to the area. The 3/502nd commander Lieutenant Colonel Robert Cole quickly realized that control of the Best vicinity would require his additional companies. Within two days, another battalion (2/502nd) would be called upon to assist.

Cole and the 3rd Battalion quickly became engaged in the woods east of Best and along roads that led to the canal and the town of Son. Lieutenant Edward Wierzbowski from Company H managed to move a small group close to the canal bridge but they were too few to seize control. The Germans blew up the bridge on the morning of the 18th. This group was subsequently cut off from the rear and the remainder of the force.

The other companies in the battalion were prevented from moving into Best and established a strong defensive position in the woods east of town. The 2/502nd moved southward towards Best on the right flank of their sister battalion. They received increasing fire as they attempted to cross a field with stands of mown hay. Some men sheltered behind the haystacks but became casualties while soldiers who continued moving forward in bursts generally succeeded. Still, the attack was halted as resistance increased. During that same day Cole stood next to his fox hole command post and was shot dead by a sniper. A lieutenant informed Major John Stopka he now commanded the battalion but could not bring himself to say the leader of the bayonet charge at Carentan had died.[7]

Lieutenant Colonel Patrick Cassidy of the 1/502nd was in the plane with division commander General Maxwell Taylor. One of the nearby transports with the divisional chief of staff aboard burst into flames. The chief of staff and other members of the parachute stick managed to jump safely but the air crew of four perished when the transport crashed. Cassidy was so distracted with concern for his men in the adjacent plane that Taylor pointed out the jump light flashing green. The battalion was responsible for the road segment near Saint-Oedenrode including a small bridge over the River Dommel. They accomplished this task on the 17th and established a defensive perimeter around the town.

By the morning of the 19th Germans near Schijndel began to move down to attack the northern end of the perimeter. Company C placed men on both sides of the road to meet the threat. By this point a temporary bridge was in place at Son and the advance of XXX Corps resumed. One of the passing Irish Guards tanks could not

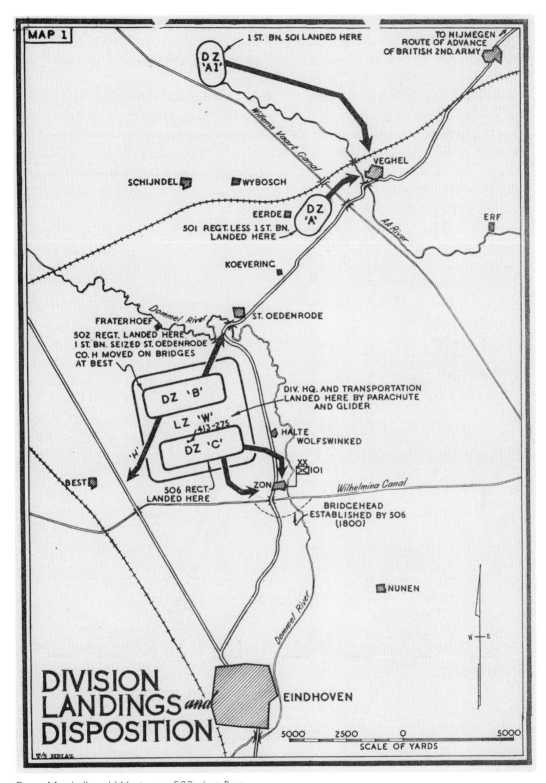

From Marshall and Westover, *502nd at Best*.

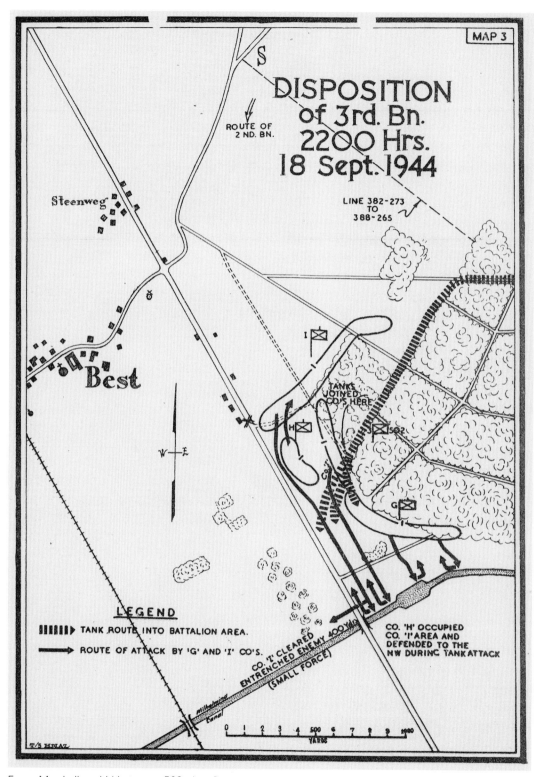

From Marshall and Westover, *502nd at Best.*

maintain column march speed due to mechanical difficulties. Cassidy asked Sergeant James 'Paddy' McRory if he would help defend the Schijndel road. The Sherman advanced along a small flank road and knocked out three 20mm cannon. Over the next few days Sergeant McRory and his tank would assist the battalion in advancing up the Schijndel road, destroying an enemy armoured car, an anti-tank gun and several enemy positions. When Cassidy praised McRory for making all the difference, he simply said, 'When in doubt, lash out.'[8]

In the vicinity of Best, time had run out for the portion of the 3/502nd with Lieutenant Wierzbowski. A mist early on the morning of the 19th masked enemy troops until they were nearly upon the group. Grenades and gunfire were exchanged. One grenade landed near Private Joe Mann, whose arms were bound in splints due to earlier wounds. He lay back upon the grenade thus saving several comrades from injury or death. Mann died a few minutes later, remembered by Wierzbowski and those comrades as the bravest man they ever knew.

The overrun group surrendered but rescue was soon at hand. Companies G and I from the battalion, British tanks and the 2/502nd Parachute Infantry moved down the woods, fields and roads to the canal and German resistance collapsed. Enemy dead numbered 600 and 1,100 prisoners were taken during the afternoon. These two battalions of the 502nd Parachute Infantry shifted northward later that day and on the 20th to assist in the defence of the part of the corridor near Saint-Oedenrode.[9]

The 1st Battalion of the 501st was led by Lieutenant Colonel Harry Kinnard who replaced the former commander killed on D-Day in Normandy. The battalion was responsible for securing crossings of the Willemsvaart canal and the River Aa near the town of Veghel and more generally defending that sector of the corridor. They staged an attack in which two companies drove defenders along the canal into the waiting arms of a third company. They defended positions in the vicinity of Eerde between Saint-Oedenrode and Veghel. Initially they faced troops from a composite force but by the end were battling elements from the German 1st and 6th Parachute Regiments with armour support. During the course of their fighting in Holland, the battalion moved in a full circle, assuming fighting orientations in all compass directions, often with exposed flanks.[10] Similar movement during the Holland operation was noted, for example, by Company E of the 506th Parachute Infantry.[11]

* * *

The 82nd Airborne Division was responsible for the middle portion of the corridor and for securing crossings over the River Maas at Grave and across the River Waal in Nijmegen. In addition, a canal connecting the two rivers presented an obstacle and planners were obsessed with seizing and maintaining control of the high ground ridges and towns east of Nijmegen. This higher ground encompassed drop and landing zones; enemy occupation of the heights could disrupt landings and prevent movement along the corridor and the Waal bridges. The forested Reichswald to the east seemed the ideal place for Germans to hide armoured forces. General Gavin decided to secure the high ground before attempting an advance on the Waal highway bridge. At the same time, he instructed Colonel Roy Lindquist to send a battalion of the 508th Parachute Infantry along the river – rather than through the congested streets of the town – to secure the highway bridge on the first evening if Lindquist thought it possible to do so.[12]

The daylight parachute landings were successful although casualties were incurred, including deaths resulting from unusual circumstances: Private Max Edmondson of 504th Parachute Infantry was struck by a bundle after landing on the drop zone. Two privates first class were lost: Curtis Morris in the 504th when his chute did not open and Peter Jasura in a quartermaster unit who fell from a transport aircraft.[13]

Troops from the 504th Parachute Infantry commanded by Colonel Reuben Tucker deployed immediately and seized the long Grave bridge across the Maas. Company E landed close to the bridge; Lieutenant John Thompson overwhelmed defensive positions on the south side. Other companies from the 504th secured the south-eastern bridge (labelled no. 7 by the division) that crossed the Maas–Waal canal near the town of Mook, but the other three bridges spanning the canal were destroyed or damaged by the Germans.[14]

The 505th Parachute Infantry landed in an open area on high ground near Groesbeek and deployed to defend the southern edge and roads leading to Nijmegen. The 508th landed to the north and assumed defensive positions on the northern edge of high ground along the road leading from Wyler through Beek and Berg en Dal into Nijmegen.

Lindquist decided movement to the Waal bridge was feasible and assigned the task to the 1/508th under Lieutenant Colonel Shields Warren. The various companies were diverted into the town on the advice of a resident apparently with the Dutch underground. They came into contact with Germans in the traffic circle at the south end of the bridge and engaged in the sort of street fighting Gavin wished to avoid. One company was cut off for several days at the main post office but did manage to destroy apparent controls for demolition charges. In response to a later query, Lindquist stated that landing along the riverside had not been possible due to the presence of anti-aircraft batteries.[15]

Another company from the 3/508th advanced along a road westward towards the bridge but encountered resistance. Unfortunately for the paratroopers and the fate of the operation, a German corps commander near Arnhem dispatched a reconnaissance battalion from the 9th SS Panzer Division southward to Nijmegen on the 17th. The battalion withdrew to a position between the Waal and Neder Rijn, but a detachment remained at the south end of the Waal bridge and those troops with reinforcements thwarted repeated efforts to gain control of the Waal crossings.

When Gavin arrived at the 508th headquarters and learned of the movement through Nijmegen he was greatly disappointed. He decided to extricate as much of the 1st Battalion as possible from the town. Those troops were needed to clear Germans from and defend the landing zone for 450 incoming gliders carrying divisional artillery, some engineers and medical personnel. The 508th and 505th troopers drove most of the enemy back to create a defensive perimeter just as the first gliders began to land in early afternoon on the 18th. Gavin later marvelled at how little equipment was lost.[16]

Leading elements of Guards Armoured Division moved quickly up the corridor from Son and established contact with the 82nd at the Maas bridge on the morning of 19 September. The Coldstream Guards assisted the 508th and part of the 505th in holding high ground and ridges. Grenadier Guards tanks and infantry aided the 2nd Battalion 505th under Lieutenant Colonel Benjamin Vandervoort in securing southern ends of the railroad and highway bridges in Nijmegen. Losses continued to mount. Lieutenant Waverly Wray and Private Herman Jacob of D/505th were among those killed on the 19th trying to approach the railroad bridge. Wray had served with the division since North Africa.[17]

The 504th moved up to the river bank on the western edge of town and prepared to cross the Waal in boats. The 3rd Battalion under Major Julian Cook assisted by Company C from the 307th Airborne Engineers would seize the northern ends of the bridges. Companies from the 1st Battalion served as reinforcements in subsequent crossings while the 2nd Battalion provided covering fire. The tanks of the Irish Guards along the river bank would fire smoke shells, machine guns and high explosive artillery. The crossing was intended for the evening of the 19th but delays in moving up XXX Corps boats due to massive traffic jams along the single road meant the crossing would not take place until three o'clock in the afternoon of the 20th.

Just as the crossing was about to begin, Gavin was called back to the high ground to direct troops against a major German attack coming from multiple directions, principally the Reichswald that had been a concern from the outset. The Germans were beginning attacks to sever the road corridor. Positions were pushed back but restored at Mook by the 505th with assistance from the Coldstream Guards armoured battalion. The 508th lost the town of Beek but held the ridge line near Berg en Dal. The commander of the 3/508, Lieutenant Colonel Louis Mendez, told Gavin they held by moving platoons from one endangered spot to another along the line.[18]

Meanwhile the 3/504th was poised for the daylight assault across the Waal. Companies H and I were assigned to the initial wave of boats while Company G followed after the boats returned. Objectives focused on the northern ends of the Waal bridges and a point further north where the railroad and highway crossed in the village of Lent. The 1/504th would cross later and form a defensive position on the north-west or left flank of the 3rd Battalion. Seven boats were lost when an exposed truck was struck by artillery fire, so soldiers would cross in the remaining twenty-seven canvas boats, with each carrying between thirteen and sixteen plus the crew of three engineers.[19]

Irish Guards tanks provided a smoke screen for fifteen minutes that soon dispersed after the first wave set out just after 3.00pm on the 20th. The tanks maintained machine gun and cannon fire to such an extent that ammunition ran low before two hours had passed and some of the machine guns became so hot they could not stop firing.[20]

Water churned from direct and plunging fire on the exposed small flotilla of canvas boats. The railroad bridge defences closest to the crossing point presented the most troublesome fire. An engineer crossing the span the next day counted thirty-four machine guns, two 20mm cannon and an 88mm gun. Approximately half of the boats were able to return for the second wave and some of those held wounded or dead soldiers. One boat hit by fire near the north shore lost a passenger overboard. Private Joseph Jedlicka sank 8 feet to the bottom with his BAR and ammunition belts. He walked along the river bottom holding his breath until surfacing on the flat shore.[21]

British commanders were in awe of the courage and fortitude displayed during the crossing. Horrocks and Browning described it as the most gallant assault they witnessed in the war; Lieutenant Colonel Gilles Vandeleur who commanded the 2/Irish Guards noted those soldiers whose boats landed simply jumped out without hesitation and moved across the flat shore inland to the dyke as the surviving boats returned for more soldiers.[22] Company C of 307th Engineers lost eight killed and twenty-seven wounded during all six crossings, including Sergeant William Kero, Corporal James Jacobs and Privates Edward Henschler, Robert Opacich, Herbert Wendland and James Woods.

The soldiers of 3rd Battalion pressed inland across the lowland flats to an elevated dyke. Some advanced to subdue opposition within the old fortification Hof van Holland while others moved along the dyke and road to the northern ends of both the railroad and highway bridges. The Americans recalled, 'prisoners were streaming back to the rear by the hundreds; hundreds of other Germans lay dead and dying.' Enemy dead reported on the railroad bridge numbered 267. One company estimated 200 to 300 enemy were killed near the junction of the railroad and highway to the north and 48 dead were spread along the railroad embankment north of the junction.[23]

Losses in the 3rd Battalion included twenty-eight killed, one missing and seventy-eight wounded during the crossings and in subsequent fighting on the northern shore around the bridges or along the northern perimeter. Lieutenant Harry Busby and Privates Dale Campbell, Thadeus Gondela, Raymond Grummer, Paul Katonik and Robert Koelle were among those lost in crossing the Waal. Occupation of Lent or fighting along the railroad embankment or the Grift dyke leading northward claimed others, including Staff Sergeant James Allen, Privates Walter Muszynski, Robert Washko (1st Battalion), Robert Wilson and Frederick Zentgraf.[24]

Company B crossed the Waal and landed just before 5.00pm. They reached the north end of the railroad bridge approximately three hours later, to find a confused mixture of men from five companies. A platoon with Lieutenant Meerman arrived at the highway bridge to join fellow paratroopers about an hour later. Companies of the 1st Battalion entered the bridgehead line from the railroad extending to the west.[25]

Continued attacks in the town of Nijmegen by the 505th and Grenadier Guards tanks finally overcame resolute German defences at the southern end of the railroad bridge and the Huner Park position surrounding a medieval fort at the south end of the highway bridge. Among the soldiers lost near the highway bridge on the 20th were Captain Robert Rosen, Private Harold Peterman and others in Companies E and F.[26]

Horrocks could barely watch at around 7.00pm as a troop of Grenadier tanks led by Sergeant Robinson set out across the bridge, since many thought the Germans would blow the bridge to pieces.[27] They did not, due to plans of Field Marshal Model to use the bridge in a counter-attack, but also quite possibly to Dutch resistance sabotage and perhaps destruction of controls in the main post office. Whatever the reason, the Grenadier tanks moved across in one of the most dramatic events of a day already filled with drama. After dark, infantry from the 3rd Battalion Irish Guards moved into the northern bridgehead.[28] The road to the Neder Rijn and the 1st British Airborne Division in Arnhem seemed at last to be open.

(**Above**) James Gavin briefed officers of 82nd Airborne Division and Army Air Corps at Cottesmore before the Operation Market jump on 17 September. Gavin assumed command of the division and the rank of major general on promotion of Matthew Ridgway to head the XVIII Airborne Corps. (*NARA*)

(**Opposite, above**) 82nd Airborne paratroopers boarding transport planes at Cottesmore airdrome photographed by Edgren on 17 September. (*NARA*)

(**Opposite, below**) 82nd Airborne boarding transports for Market on 17 September. (*NARA*)

(**Above**) Meyer photographed Gavin checking equipment near his transport before take-off. *(NARA)*

(**Opposite, above**) Meyer later recorded most of the members of the 'stick' or plane load of eighteen troopers. General Gavin stood near the head of the group. *(NARA)*

(**Opposite, below**) Troops from the 101st Airborne Division march towards transport planes. The photograph was recorded by Klosterman and dated 18 September when gliders carrying artillery and support troops arrived. Since no gliders were attached to the C-47s the scene may show a parachute regiment on the first day of the operation. *(NARA)*

377589

(**Opposite, above**) A classic portrait by Gloster of Major General Maxwell Taylor who commanded the 101st Airborne as he boarded a transport plane bound for Holland on 17 September. (*NARA*)

(**Opposite, below**) American paratroopers aboard a transport plane en route to Holland on the 17th. Since Meyer recorded this photo and the earlier ones of Gavin, this group may be a portion of the general's stick or at least were members of the 82nd. (*NARA*)

(**Above**) Tischler photographed transports in the air with fighter planes providing protection overhead on the 17th Numerous paratroopers were descending on a drop zone. (*NARA*)

(**Above**) Another photograph by Tischler showed parachutes billowing below the transport aircraft above their drop zone. (*NARA*)

(**Opposite, above**) A remarkable series of images by a photographer who jumped during the operation on the 17th. The density of open parachutes was readily apparent during the descent. (*NARA*)

(**Opposite, below**) Transport planes were visible above the descending paratroopers. (*NARA*)

354700

(**Above**) One unfortunate parachutist landed upside down near a haystack in a Dutch field. (*NARA*)

(**Opposite, above**) Numerous paratroopers descending and one running to his assembly point. The drop zone, variously identified as near Son for the 101st or near Groesbeek for the 82nd, is uncertain since these Army Signal Corps contact prints do not provide a specific location. (*NARA*)

(**Opposite, below**) A wooded location that probably contained concealed German positions along the route of advance. The view was recorded along Berkheuvels west of the Valkenswaard road.

The field of fire from the general area of German positions facing south-east to the Valkenswaard road, route of advance for the Irish Guards on the afternoon of 17 September.

Grave marker at Valkenswaard War Cemetery for Squadron Sergeant Major W. Parkes of the 2nd Battalion Irish Guards killed during the opening advance of the Garden phase.

C-47 tow planes and gliders arranged on a runway before take-off for Holland, photographed by Edgren on 18 September. *(NARA)*

(**Above**) Meyer captured an image of gliders crossing the English coast en route to Holland on the 18th. (*NARA*)

(**Opposite, above**) Gliders landing near Son probably carrying the 327th Glider Infantry from the 101st as photographed by Jones on 18 September. (*NARA*)

(**Opposite, below**) Jones photographed one of the gliders that crashed on landing the same day. Soldiers assisted casualties from the rough landing. (*NARA*)

194180-5

(**Above**) Klosterman recorded the unloading of a glider in a turnip field with civilians nearby on the 18th. (*NARA*)

(**Opposite, above**) Klosterman photographed an act of generosity as Private Bernard Nakla from the 101st offered chewing gum to a young Dutch girl on the 18th probably near the glider landing area. (*NARA*)

(**Opposite, below**) Dutch civilians with a group of 101st soldiers including a radio operator photographed by Jones on the 18th. (*NARA*)

195095

SIGNAL CORPS U.S. ARMY

(**Above**) The landing zone for the 502nd and 506th Parachute Infantry Regiments south of Saint-Oedenrode photographed at sunset.

(**Opposite, above**) An unpaved lane along the edge of a woods within the perimeter defended by the 3rd Battalion 502nd Parachute Infantry near Best from 17 through 19 September.

(**Opposite, below left**) Lieutenant Colonel Robert Cole, known as the hero of Carentan, was killed near the 3/502nd command post on 18 September. (*NARA*)

(**Opposite, below right**) Private Joe Mann, the bravest man his fellow soldiers ever knew, died on 19 September. (*NARA*)

(**Above**) The local population welcoming elements of the 101st upon their entry to Eindhoven as seen by Jones on 18 September. *(NARA)*

(**Opposite, above**) After a temporary bridge had been constructed over the Wilhelmina canal in Son, leading elements of the Guards Armoured Division continued their advance up the corridor to Grave and Nijmegen. Jones photographed a portion of the crossing on the 19th. *(NARA)*

(**Opposite, below**) The current bridge across the Wilhelmina canal at Son photographed facing north, the opposite direction from the 1944 image.

195099

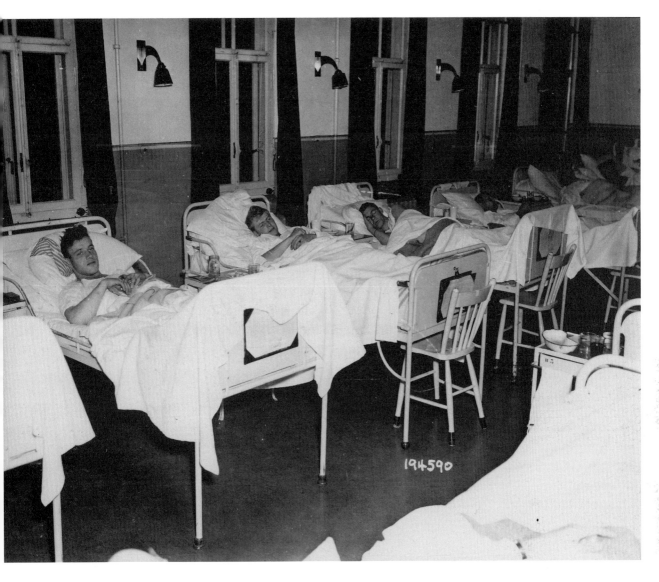

(**Opposite, above**) The landing zone for the 508th Parachute Infantry near Groesbeek facing east.

(**Opposite, below**) The Maas bridge at Grave seized by the 504th Parachute Infantry on 17 September. The photograph shows the view from south-east of the bridge.

(**Above**) Some wounded from the 82nd Airborne received care in a Nijmegen hospital. (*NARA*)

Three women view the grave of Private Harold Peterman from Company F 505th Parachute Infantry killed by artillery fire on Oranjesingel in Nijmegen on 20 September while assaulting the Waal highway bridge (Thuring and Heij, *Verdwenen Kerkhoven*). Poznak recorded the scene on the following day. *(NARA)*

Another photograph by Poznak on the 21st showed the same group of women probably near the grave of Private Peterman as 82nd Airborne soldiers passed. *(NARA)*

A dead German soldier lying in a Nijmegen street with a Guards Armoured tank in the background. Poznak recorded the photograph on 20 September. *(NARA)*

(**Above**) Wounded Germans surrender to the British in Nijmegen on the 21st in a photograph by Poznak. *(NARA)*

(**Opposite, above**) Poznak encountered citizens accused of collaboration rounded up by Dutch resistance on the 21st. *(NARA)*

(**Opposite, below**) Dutch collaborators in Nijmegen on the previous day, photographed by Poznak. *(NARA)*

The highway bridge spanning the River Waal viewed from the current railroad bridge.

A view of the Waal highway bridge facing south-east from a dyke on the north bank, a position occupied by 3/504th on 20 September. The high ground near Groesbeek south-east of Nijmegen is clearly visible behind the bridge.

Chapter Six

'Not one shall be forgotten'

The 1st British Airborne Division was scheduled to land near Arnhem over a period of three days. The first lift on 17 September carried 1st Parachute Brigade, 1st Airlanding Brigade and divisional troops including reconnaissance, artillery and anti-tank batteries and the headquarters of Major General Robert 'Roy' Urquhart. The parachute and glider landings were almost perfect but occurred on zones 6 to 8 miles west of the Neder Rijn bridge in Arnhem. Since opposition was expected to be minimal, the distance was not considered an obstacle. The three battalions in 1st Parachute Brigade organized quickly and began long marches to the bridge on three separate routes. The Airlanding Brigade remained to hold and defend a drop zone for 4th Parachute Brigade and other divisional units arriving next day. The shortage of transport aircraft was a major limiting factor.

These components of the division undertook the first two elements of the operational plan. Once the landings on 18 September occurred, the 1st Airlanding Brigade would move to form a defensive barrier on the western edge of Arnhem. The 4th Parachute Brigade after landing was expected to extend the line on the northern high ground and connect with the 1st Parachute Brigade along a primary road leading north from the town. The Polish Parachute Brigade commanded by Major General Stanisław Sosobowski was scheduled to land on 19 September south of the Neder Rijn bridge. Those troops were to form a barrier on the eastern end of town after they crossed the bridge expected to be in British hands.[1]

Two battalions advancing into Arnhem were partially turned back but the 2nd Battalion led by Lieutenant Colonel John Frost continued to move through Oosterbeek and along the river road. The battalion sought to secure the northern end of the railroad bridge but it was blown up practically in their faces. The column had a sharp engagement on the road underpass beneath the railroad with an armoured car and supporting infantry. They finally reached the Neder Rijn bridge in Arnhem by early evening and established defensive positions in buildings around the north end. They were unable to dislodge Germans from the south end. The British at the north end were reinforced by platoons from 3rd Battalion and headquarters troops from 1st Brigade. During the morning of the 18th, additional soldiers from 2nd Battalion, some engineers and a troop of 6-pounder anti-tank guns arrived and were positioned in a defence arc around the north end composed of 600 to 700 men.

Later in the morning a German armoured reconnaissance column attempted to cross from the south bank. These troops had moved to Nijmegen the previous day, crossing the Neder Rijn bridge en route before Lieutenant Colonel Frost's troops arrived. The column was halted on the bridge and about ten vehicles were destroyed by 6-pounders or Piat rounds. Late in the day the defensive position was attacked from the north bank but held following house to house fighting that drove off two German tanks.[2]

The 1st Airborne headquarters received various forms of bad news shortly after landing. Reconnaissance jeeps intended to move quickly into town had been stopped. Opposition between the landing zones was building, initially from local defence troops but later from not one but two SS panzer divisions under command of General Willi Bittrich of II SS Panzer Corps. In addition, Field Marshal Walter Model who commanded Army Group B was present in a headquarters within Oosterbeek. Due to problems with radio communications, General Urquhart went forward to check on progress in the late afternoon of the 17th. The general did not return on the 18th and no word was received from him, so Brigadier Philip 'Pip' Hicks from 1st Airlanding Brigade assumed command. This situation obtained when the 4th Parachute Brigade of Brigadier John Hackett landed on the afternoon of the 18th.

A Dutch liaison officer informed 1st Airborne headquarters around 3.00pm on the 18th that parachute companies occupied houses at the north end of the bridge. The report was reinforced by a forward artillery observer the following afternoon.[3] Although communication both within and beyond Arnhem was limited by radio difficulties, some word of the problems confronting 1st Airborne was coming out via the Dutch underground. By midday on the 18th, the 82nd informed its regiments that the Dutch reported German forces were gaining the upper hand.[4]

General Urquhart returned early on the 19th to announce that Brigadier Gerald Lathbury of 1st Brigade had been wounded and remained in town. The division commander learned the true nature of the opposition deployed against them.

The 1st Airborne made no headway in attempts to reach the bridge. Events on the morning of the 19th provide a stark example. The 2nd South Staffords (1st Airlanding Brigade) and 11th Parachute Battalion began to advance into the city. Remnants of 1st and 3rd Parachute Battalions were simultaneously moving along the river road. The South Staffords advanced towards the high ground and expended the balance of their Piat ammunition against an armoured attack that still broke through. The South Staffords withdrew to an anti-tank screen to aid 11th Parachute but were mortared and again overrun by tanks.

The planned effort by 11th Parachute was also disrupted by tanks that earlier overran the South Staffords' position. Those remaining troops from these two battalions fell back to a position near the ancient Oosterbeek church. They joined soldiers from 1st and 3rd Battalions to form a composite group known famously as 'Lonsdale Force' after Major R. Lonsdale of 11th Battalion. Casualties had been so heavy among the four battalions that Lonsdale Force contained the equivalent of less than one battalion, only 400 men and eight 6-pounder anti-tank guns.[5]

Lieutenant Colonel Frost and his small group were isolated for the balance of their time at the bridge. The remainder of the division began by 20 September to form an irregular roughly thumb-shaped pocket in Oosterbeek with its base or rear opening on the Neder Rijn.

General Bittrich divided his corps units shortly after the parachute landings. The 9th SS Division would focus on airborne forces north of the Neder Rijn while 10th SS would move to the Nijmegen area to reinforce troops holding the Waal bridges. Bittrich implored Model to permit demolition of the Waal highway bridge but this the Field Marshal refused to do. These divisions survived the Normandy debacle with relatively little armoured equipment intact. Their movement to the Arnhem area was intended to provide an opportunity to rest and replace the mechanized equipment on which a panzer division was so dependent.

These two divisions in II SS Panzer Corps had few tanks but did have self-propelled assault guns, armoured half-tracks and artillery batteries in addition to infantry battalions. Earlier in the year the divisions fought in Crimea and since late June in Normandy. Those veterans who survived were dedicated soldiers not for the most part tainted by the atrocities associated with other SS divisions. In the coming fight they would behave largely in a correct manner, possibly due to the leadership of Bittrich. Since the 1st Airborne quickly realized the matter at hand was no less than survival of their division, the stage was set for bitter and ferocious fighting at close quarters resulting in the destruction of much of Arnhem and Oosterbeek.

*   *   *

Colonel Tucker of the 504th Parachute Infantry was furious at the north end of the Waal highway bridge on the evening of 20 September. The Grenadier Guards tank squadron that crossed the bridge paused as Tucker's men formed a northern perimeter. The tanks lacked infantry support although members of the 3rd Battalion Irish Guards moved across at night to assume responsibility for close protection of the bridge.[6] Tucker had an angry confrontation with squadron officers who informed him the Grenadiers had been ordered not to advance along the raised and exposed road to Arnhem that evening without infantry support. Gavin later expressed strong objections to Horrocks.[7]

Although no one outside Arnhem knew for certain – not troops on the banks of the Waal and not even 1st Airborne headquarters in Oosterbeek – the gallant band of airborne troops were finally driven from the north end of the bridge in Arnhem. The survivors and their wounded surrendered early next morning, 21 September.

British commanders ordered an advance early that morning and so informed the 1st Airborne.[8] Irish Guards tanks crossed the Waal to find their sister battalion 'was not expecting them'. By 11.00am the Irish Guards group was ordered to advance up the main highway past the railroad junction towards the town of Elst and ultimately to the Neder Rijn. Artillery fire was laid down on a road leading east to the town of Ressen; enemy positions were thought present behind the road in adjoining orchards.

The Guards advanced only a few miles when three leading tanks were struck and put out of action by German guns. The column stopped and attempted to call down air support, but faulty communications initially prevented contact. Then they were informed that Allied aircraft were held to either protect or avoid contact with transport planes bringing the Polish Parachute Brigade to a drop zone south of the Neder Rijn. The Welsh Guards in support attempted to move around to the left with no success.

Infantry sought protection in deep ditches while the tanks could not move off the dyke into the fields. Enemy artillery and mortar fire continued through the afternoon. Around 6.00pm the group retired about 1,000 yards. A few days later they moved past Ressen and discovered residue suggesting the road orchard positions had been held by numerous 75mm guns and two 88mm guns. They saw debris from perhaps an infantry company and track marks of a Tiger tank that had withdrawn after being struck by a 17-pounder shell from a Sherman Firefly tank.

Shortly after the battle the Irish Guards learned that Dutch Staff College students were asked how one should attack Arnhem from Nijmegen. If the candidate suggested moving up the main road through Elst he would not be promoted. If he chose to move west and approach the river through Driel he would become a colonel. Colonel Joe later thought the western route, though a long way around, was preferable to the elevated road flanked by ditches, a route completely unsuited for armour. They had, however, been ordered to advance straight up the main road.[9]

During the evening of the 21st or early on the 22nd, reconnaissance armoured cars from the Household Cavalry followed the western route through Oosterhout and at last reached the Neder Rijn near Driel where they made contact with Polish airborne troopers. Then began a series of night attempts to transport sufficient troops across the river into the airborne perimeter at Oosterbeek. Fifty Poles crossed on the night of the 22/23rd followed by about 200 to 250 the following evening, too few to change the outcome on the north shore. The first time they were conveyed in small rubber rafts that could only carry a few men and came under devastating enemy fire when illuminated by flares. On the second attempt they used those surviving canvas boats that had carried the 504th across the Waal.[10]

The 43rd Infantry Division managed the difficult task of moving up the crowded road corridor and attempted to advance past German defences on the road to Elst. Horrocks was determined to make one more effort to reach the airborne troops in Oosterbeek. The 4th Dorsets from the 43rd Division and the Polish Brigade would try another crossing on the night of 24/25th. The canvas boats were transferred to the Dorsets when it was decided to scale back the size of the assault. The Poles were not subjected to a third attempt and the Dorsets sent only 400 soldiers and twenty officers. The transfer of the canvas boats delayed the effort and opposition on the north bank prevented the Dorsets from assembling into an effective force; only some of them managed to reach the airborne perimeter.[11] The approach of XXX Corps did bring batteries of artillery within range to support the airborne troops. Urquhart marvelled at the accuracy of this gunfire on German positions and believed the artillery support may have saved what remained of his division.

Additional problems arose further south on the corridor. The 107th Panzer Brigade sought to cut the corridor at the reconstructed Son bridge as early as the 19th; they seized the area at 6.00pm but the 506th Parachute Infantry regained control about three hours later. A more serious threat emerged on the 22nd during a concerted effort to destroy several crossings in the sector near Veghel and Uden. The 101st battled the 107th Panzer Brigade on the east side with the 59th Division attacking from the west along several miles of roadway. Portions of Company E of the 506th were isolated in each town when the corridor was overrun south of Uden. Despite artillery poundings their positions held with assistance from elements of Guards Armoured Division sent south by Horrocks. These units fought into Veghel on the 23rd but the vital supply line along the road had been stopped for a day.[12]

The Garden plan called for support from two other British corps, VIII to the east and XII along the west. Both encountered strong resistance and had not kept pace. VIII Corps on the right was delayed along the Willemsvaart canal and later between Helmond and Deurne east of Son. Their movement did compel 107th Panzer Brigade to fall back from the corridor. XII Corps on the left met stout resistance for two days south of the Wilhelmina canal and then fought five more days to move through the town of Best where the 502nd Parachute Infantry earlier held a line.[13]

Horrocks remained determined to achieve a meaningful assault crossing but General Miles Dempsey in command of the British Second Army thought otherwise. The reopened corridor was cut again on the evening of the 24th between Saint-Oedenrode and the canal at Veghel. Browning felt the crossing plan was overly optimistic and so informed Dempsey. After discussion with Horrocks and receiving Montgomery's approval, Dempsey decided to withdraw those troops who could do so back across the Neder Rijn near Driel. The withdrawal occurred on the rainy night of 25–26 September. Most of the wounded and medical personnel remained, including some walking wounded who agreed to man trenches to cover the retreat.

The canvas boats were brought forward again and carried as many as possible to the south bank under the cover of darkness. By daylight several hundred still remained and some attempted to swim across the river. The 1st British Airborne Division landed 8,905 soldiers and about 1,100 glider pilots near Arnhem. The boats largely enabled 2,163 to cross the river, in addition to about 160 Poles and 75 Dorsets who entered the perimeter only a few days earlier.[14]

*   *   *

No one knew the limits of airborne warfare but they clearly had been exceeded during Market Garden. The outcome many feared during previous airborne operations came to pass: an entire division landed too far away to be reached by ground forces and, thus cut off, was largely destroyed by the enemy.

Criticism was directed at many individuals in the months and years following the end of the operation and made for moving reading. Most sources agree the British airborne zones were located much too far away from the Arnhem road bridge; both Urquhart and Montgomery accepted responsibility for not challenging the RAF zone placements. Urquhart discovered a battalion could have landed south of the bridge despite pessimistic evaluations provided to him. Certainly the narrow corridor of advance vulnerable to attack from three sides would only have succeeded against weak and collapsing opposition. The quality of the German opposition particularly the presence of two SS panzer divisions near Arnhem was a decisive factor.

The official British military history found fault with the drop zone locations and Urquhart's decisions to advance along distinctly separate routes and leave his headquarters during the crucial early days. Urquhart responded that the various battalions could not offer mutual support in built-up areas so multiple routes would maximize chances for success.[15] He recognized some blame might be attached to his movement forward so early in the battle, but he did not anticipate the radio problems.

The commanders of 1st British Airborne Division and XXX Corps saw the event very differently. Urquhart was convinced XXX Corps had not shown sufficient drive or determination during its advance, especially after crossing the Waal at Nijmegen. Horrocks for his part accepted responsibility for the pace of movement but rejected any suggestion by those 'who should have known better' that 43rd Division had advanced too slowly.[16]

In the immediate aftermath of the operation, Browning and Montgomery directed harsh criticism at General Sosobowski, a sceptic of the undertaking from the beginning. The Polish Brigade had demanded to be flown to Warsaw in August to assist in the general uprising and considered a hunger strike when denied the opportunity. The general did not enjoy warm relations with his British commanders and following numerous delays threatened to withdraw his brigade from the 21 September jump unless accurate information was provided on conditions near Arnhem.[17] Despite the

Polish general's 'renowned independence' Urquhart later thought the decision to place the Polish Brigade under command of a brigadier in the 43rd Division during a planned assault across the Neder Rijn did not show sufficient respect for Sosobowski or his brigade. At any rate Lieutenant Colonel Charles Mackenzie from the 1st Airborne who heard the assault planning knew the intended force was insufficient to offer any meaningful help.[18]

If as seems probable the general was a scapegoat to deflect attention from the failure of Market Garden, such motives do not reflect well on the reputations of Browning or Montgomery. Furthermore, the overall performance of the Polish Parachute Brigade was questioned as Churchill was attempting to enlist the Polish government-in-exile in his 'negotiations' of Poland's postwar boundaries with the Soviets. Sosobowski was removed from command of the brigade in late 1944. He remained a member of the *émigré* community in England rather than return to a country dominated by the Communists and died in London as Cornelius Ryan was preparing *A Bridge Too Far*. That book and other sources greatly served to rehabilitate the reputations of the Polish paratroopers and their former commander who remain honoured figures in the town of Driel.

Montgomery supported the operation's concept for years to come. He thought the effort would have succeeded with more supplies and transport despite his own mistakes, the presence of German forces in Arnhem and elsewhere, and the appalling weather that grounded several follow-up reinforcement and supply missions. He remained an 'unrepentant advocate' of Market Garden.[19]

The Americans engaged in a degree of criticism or at least re-evaluation. Eisenhower 'insisted' on the undertaking[20] when it was proposed by Montgomery and was obviously disappointed in the outcome. He believed the supply limitations surrounding the entire operation emphasized the importance of opening the port of Antwerp.

Gavin described the operation in early October 1944 as 'A very marginal performance and one that will not be duplicated in this war. The perfect airborne show.'[21] By July 1945 he responded more positively to Captain Westover: 'Those of us who participated in the operation consider it a model airborne show ... The 82d Airborne Division's participation in MARKET was well conceived and very well planned considering the short time available (6 days). The mechanics of its execution were almost perfect.' He justified the focus on the high ground over the Waal bridge on the initial day.[22]

The official American history emphasized problems occasioned by weather and intelligence failures to recognize that the true nature of German opposition might still have been overcome except for delays south of Eindhoven, the Son bridge and the Waal crossing in Nijmegen.[23] Ambrose emphasized the hazards of such an operation on a narrow front. As a consequence Allied airborne forces at times failed to capture or hold certain bridges or the long corridor despite the obvious quality of those forces.[24]

The 82nd held the line east of Nijmegen extending just into Germany and in the low lying ground referred to as the 'island' between the Waal and Neder Rijn. The 101st Airborne also moved from the southern end of the corridor into the island. Continued occupation of these lines was boring, miserable and dangerous. The 101st lost 2,110 men in Market Garden and another 1,682 during the remaining time in Holland. Losses in the 82nd numbered 1,432 during the first nine or ten days; an additional 1,912 casualties were sustained during the 'defensive' phase lasting into mid-November.[25] The 326th Medical Company (101st Airborne Division) treated more than 3,000 casualties during the campaign, 2,653 of them being American soldiers. The remainder were Allies, civilians and enemy prisoners. The company noted in particular the impact of the German Schu mine that resulted 'in deeper shock than any other type of casualty during the entire operation' due to traumatic removal of the leg below the knee.[26]

Problems related to looting of Dutch homes were reported and investigated by both divisions. The 101st decided on 24 October to relieve one company commander and admonish or formally reprimand five battalion commanders and another company commander. Legal charges were filed against two soldiers, while the 501st undertook less severe action against others.[27] Gavin noted 'the looting problem is in hand I believe,' although reports continued in early November. The inspector general from Supreme Allied Headquarters visited the 82nd but the division was not considered at fault. Gavin noted accusations originated with the group around General Krules, the 'older reactionaries' vying for political power with the younger element favouring Prince Bernhard.[28]

Prospects appeared bleaker in early November. The enemy defences on the front became tougher and patrols sent out were losing men without the compensation of taking prisoners. Gavin complained bitterly he had 'the best offensive troops in the theatre and we sit in fox holes for two months'. Still some humour remained. It had been reported the Germans were using dogs, so the 504th 'rounded up the most attractive bitches in Nijmegen. Results uncertain.'[29] Months later he would learn more stories about the regiment, including their supposed technique during the campaign near Nijmegen of pulling Germans out of fox holes then dropping the smaller ones back in with grenades.[30]

The 82nd was relieved by a Canadian division in mid-November. Gavin lamented it was 'heartbreaking to completely abandon this salient that we have given so many lives to obtain'.[31] The division returned to quarters in France, followed shortly afterward by soldiers of the 101st.

Paratroopers from the 1st British Airborne Division aboard a plane bound for drop zones west of Arnhem on 17 September. The photographer, Poznak, evidently exposed the image before take-off since he was later with the 82nd Airborne in Nijmegen on 20 and 21 September. (*NARA*)

De parachutisten landen bij Arnhem

Drawing of airborne operations by 8-year-old resident, now on display at Airborne Museum in former Hartenstein Hotel in Oosterbeek.

(**Opposite, above**) View of polder land north of the Neder Rijn in Oosterbeek with current railroad bridge in background. Polder land considered unsuitable for glider landings before the operation bordered the river road along which members of the 2nd Parachute Battalion marched into Arnhem.

(**Opposite, below**) The railroad overpass under which the river road led to Arnhem.

(**Above**) As British airborne troops passed through the overpass they encountered fire from an impromptu German position on raised ground beyond the overpass. The southern brick abutment still bears impact scars from this gun fire on the 17th.

(**Above**) Graves at Arnhem Oosterbeek War Cemetery. Sergeant D.C. Follington, aged 26, a British glider pilot killed on 17 September and Lieutenant S.E. Watling, aged 28, from the Parachute Regiment killed on 19 September.

(**Right**) Journalists and army photographers who landed with the 1st Airborne compiled a remarkable catalogue of dispatches and images of those who defended the Oosterbeek perimeter. Sergeant D.M. Smith viewed Company C of 1st Battalion The Border Regiment holding the line along Van Lennepweg on 21 September. German troops were positioned roughly 100 yards away. (*IWM*)

(**Opposite**) View of Driel from a dyke to the south. After several delays in England due to poor weather, portions of the Polish Parachute Brigade jumped south of the Neder Rijn near this village on 21 September.

194336-S

(**Opposite, above**) The 2nd Battalion Irish Guards moved across the Waal highway bridge in an attempt to reach the Neder Rijn and Arnhem on the 21st. The ubiquitous photographer Poznak recorded the scene as the Sherman *Buncrana* from B Squadron led a troop across the bridge. The long barrel indicated *Buncrana* mounted a 17-pounder gun and was known as a Firefly. The netting visible on the barrel when deployed served to disguise this fact from German gunners. Since only one tank in each troop of four mounted this formidable gun, the Firefly presented a preferred target. (*NARA*)

(**Opposite, below**) View from the German position along the road to Ressen facing the line of advance of the Irish Guards on 21 September. The elevation of the corridor is still indicated by the visibility of modern traffic moving along the road.

(**Above**) The stream of traffic moving north across the Waal highway bridge photographed by Poznak on 21 September. (*NARA*)

(**Opposite, above left**) Grave at Arnhem Oosterbeek of Guardsman A.M. Murphy, aged 28, of the Irish Guards killed on 21 September.

(**Opposite, above right**) Private John Towle from Ohio, aged 20, assisted Company C 504th Parachute Infantry along the defensive perimeter north of the bridge. He fired on and stopped a tank in Oosterhout. Private Towle later received the Medal of Honor for the efforts that claimed his life on 21 September. (*NARA*)

(**Opposite, below**) Poor weather prevented troops of the 325th Glider Infantry from arriving to reinforce the 82nd Airborne east of Nijmegen until 23 September. Tischler exposed this photograph as the gliders were towed to Holland on either 23 or 24 September. (*NARA*)

(**Above**) Morton recorded gliders on the landing zone and planes dropping parachutes on the 23rd. The parachutists were likely remaining members of the Polish Parachute Brigade who were unable to jump due to weather conditions on the 21st and were finally deployed east of Nijmegen two days later. (*NARA*)

One of the gliders that crashed on the 23rd; all of the occupants escaped. (*NARA*)

A glider landing zone photographed by Heibonstret on the 23rd with a C-47 tow plane falling to the ground in the background. (*NARA*)

A few seconds later the same photographer recorded the erupting fireball from the tow plane crash. *(NARA)*

German attacks severed the central portion of the corridor between Veghel and Uden on the 23rd. Jones recorded a Panther knocked out of action during the fighting in Erp east of Veghel. *(NARA)*

195211

(**Opposite, above**) The British also lost armour that day in Erp. Jones photographed an incapacitated Sherman Firefly on the 23rd. (*NARA*)

(**Above**) General Miles Dempsey, commander of the British Second Army, at 101st Airborne headquarters on the 23rd. Supply movement was disrupted for a day along the road corridor. Dempsey considered withdrawing airborne forces from the Oosterbeek perimeter north of the Neder Rijn. (*NARA*)

(**Opposite, below**) The corridor became increasingly difficult to navigate as attested by the traffic and wrecked vehicles photographed on 25 September. (*NARA*)

195212

195213

(**Opposite, above**) A British tank passed a dead Luftwaffe soldier, probably a member of a parachute regiment, on the 25th. (*NARA*)

(**Opposite, below**) A British Sherman destroyed and the crew killed along the corridor photographed on the 26th. (*NARA*)

(**Above**) Grave at Arnhem Oosterbeek of Kapral Tadeusz Koszela, aged 29, from the 2nd Batalion Spadochronowy in the Polish Parachute Brigade killed on 25 September.

Norbie witnessed the evacuation of a Dutch family from Kerkrade on the German border during the same day, 25 September. Most residents of Arnhem and Oosterbeek were compelled by Germans to evacuate in retaliation for the Market operation. Many were relocated by the Dutch government to the north of Holland. *(NARA)*

Poznak photographed the aftermath of an air raid on 29 October: an ambulance from the 101st Airborne burned on a street. (NARA)

Paratroopers of all sorts jumped during Market Garden, including a dog belonging to Private Peter Barenowski of the 506th Parachute Infantry. Jones immortalized the loyal mascot on 17 October. (NARA)

(**Above**) Troopers from the 82nd began to depart Nijmegen after relief by Canadian troops. Although the photograph by Lynch was marked October, many of the airborne troops remained in Holland until the last weeks of November. (*NARA*)

(**Opposite**) Nijmegen was the mistaken target of an Allied air raid before Market Garden but more damage arose from attempts to seize the Waal bridges and German air raids following the operation. These views were photographed by Poznak on 28 September. (*NARA*)

(**Above**) The scope of damage to the town was reflected by this view in late September or October. The district suffered from heavy fighting to capture the Waal highway bridge. (*NARA*)

(**Opposite, above**) A modern view of the Waal highway bridge from the municipal park high ground.

(**Opposite, below**) Many of the 101st casualties found temporary resting places in a cemetery near Son. Smart photographed the site near the corner of Plot C on 24 February 1945. (*NARA*)

(**Above**) Dutch children adopted the graves of Allied soldiers, a tradition that continues today. Tipton photographed the Memorial Day ceremony in Son on 30 May 1948. (*NARA*)

(**Opposite, above**) The 82nd Airborne opened a cemetery at Molenhoek near the Maas–Waal canal on 20 September 1944 as the battle to secure the Waal bridges was ongoing. Hurst photographed the location during a Memorial Day commemoration on 30 May 1947. (*NARA*)

(**Opposite, below**) Eventually the Americans were either repatriated or moved from temporary burial grounds at Molenhoek, Son and other locations, to Margraten in south-east Holland that is maintained today by the American Battle Monuments Commission. Taylor photographed the Margraten cemetery on 15 May 1947. (*NARA*)

The parents of Private Joe Mann from the 502nd Parachute Infantry attended the dedication of a monument honouring his memory in the woods near Best. Mann gave his life by covering a grenade to shield comrades. He was later awarded the Medal of Honor. The photograph was taken on 17 September 1956 probably by Wasserzug. The faces still reflect the pride of soldiers, curiosity among young residents but primarily the sadness of his parents. (NARA)

The Arnhem Oosterbeek War Cemetery maintained by the Commonwealth War Graves Commission as it appeared just before the 70th commemoration in September 2014.

ZGINĘLI W AKCJI BOJOWEJ ODDALI SWE ŻYCIE
ZA WOLNĄ I NIEPODLEGŁĄ POLSKĘ
POD ARNHEM W 1944 ROKU.

ks.kapelan MISIUDA HUBERT
kpt. GAZUREK IGNACY
por. KUTRZEBA JAN
por. PUDEŁKO MIECZYSŁAW
por. RACIŚ JERZY
por. ŚLESICKI STANISŁAW
p.por. GRABOWSKI WALENTY
p.por. HORODYŃSKI BOGUSŁAW
p.por. JAWORSKI WACŁAW
p.por. KOLASIŃSKI TADEUSZ
p.por. KRUKOWSKI ZBIGNIEW
p.por. TICE RICHARD
plut.pohr. KOSTRZ EDWARD
kpr. pchr. PICHETA WACŁAW
kpr. pchr. ZJAWIN ZBIGNIEW
st.strz.pchr. OSTOJSKI TADEUSZ
st.strz.pchc. ŻEBROWSKI IGNACY
sierż. SAŁWUK ANTONI
plut. KOSSAKOWSKI JAN
plut. KĘDZIOŁA FRANCISZEK
plut. LEPALCZYK TOMASZ
plut. MORCHONOWICZ EDWARD
plut. PAWŁOWSKI STANISŁAW
kpr. ANIOŁ BOLESŁAW
kpr. BOROWIEC MIECZYSŁAW
kpr. GIENIEC JÓZEF
kpr. GRZYB ANTONI
kpr. KOSZELA TADEUSZ
kpr. PASZKO KAZIMIERZ
kpr. PLICHTA STEFAN
kpr. SINIAK MATEUSZ
kpr. TROCHIM EDWARD

kpr. ZAWISTOWSKI STEFAN
st.strz. BISIOREK ZYGMUNT
st.strz. BŁASZKO MICHAŁ
st.strz. KULIKOWSKI JAN
st.strz. GATEWNIK CZESŁAW
st.strz. HEWAK KAZIMIERZ
st.strz. JABŁOŃSKI PIOTR
st.strz. KOPEC STANISŁAW
st.strz. KOWALSKI LUCJAN
st.strz. MACHEL CZESŁAW
st.strz. MANIA BOLESŁAW
st.strz. NOWAK MARIAN
st.strz. NYCZ WALENTY
st.strz. PAŁKA WŁADYSŁAW
st.strz. SITEK STANISŁAW
st.strz. SZKWAREK JÓZEF
st.strz. TKACZYK JAN
st.sap. RODO MICHAŁ
strz. ABRAMIUK DYMITR
strz. BANAŚ BRONISŁAW
strz. BEKER FRANCISZEK
strz. BIER ANATOL
strz. BZOWY MIKOŁAJ
strz. DEC ADAM
strz. KANDA PIOTR
strz. KOZAK ŁUKASZ
strz. LICZNER ALEKSANDER
strz. LIPECKI TADEUSZ
strz. MAŚLORZ PIOTR
strz. MENTLIK EMIL
strz. MOSZOWSKI MICHAŁ
strz. NIEDŹWIECKI MICHAŁ

st.strz. BŁAŻEJEWICZ MIECZYSŁAW
st.strz. KŁAPOUCHY STANISŁAW
st.strz. KRZECZKOWSKI MIECZYSŁAW
st.strz. KUCZEWSKI WŁADYSŁAW
st.strz. WESOŁOWICZ KONSTANTY
strz. JANKIEWICZ ZDZISŁAW
strz. BURDACH STANISŁAW
strz. KORNIŁOWICZ STANISŁAW
strz. ŁUKASIEWICZ FRANCISZEK
strz. OLSZEWSKI STANISŁAW
strz. PAULSKI BOLESŁAW
strz. SKIERS WŁADYSŁAW
strz. SOSKÓW TADEUSZ
strz. SZYLAK ARTUR
strz. WIĘGEK STANISŁAW
strz. WOLBIN PIOTR
strz. ZALEWSKI TADEUSZ
strz. ŻOŁYNIAK BRONISŁAW
kan. BEDNARSKI JAN
kan. CHMIELEWSKI WIKTOR
kan. GORZKO STANISŁAW
kan. KOCAJ PIOTR
kan. NOWAK KAZIMIERZ
kan. RATOWSKI JÓZEF
kan. SOBOTA LEGIERO PAWEŁ
kan. STANDARSKI KAROL
sap. PAWLUCZUK ZYGMUNT
bomb. CHARTONOWICZ KAZIMIERZ
bomb. SKACZKO JÓZEF
bomb. WAWROS ALOJZY

R.I.P

Memorial in Driel to members of the Polish Parachute Brigade killed during Market Garden.

In September 1944 British Airborne soldiers and their Polish comrades, with the support of brave Dutch men and women, fought a grim battle around this ancient Church in the struggle to liberate the Netherlands from Nazi tyranny.

This stone commemorates all who took part in this action and above all those who died.

NOT ONE SHALL BE FORGOTTEN

Monument near the ancient church in Oosterbeek dedicated to the memories of soldiers and civilians with the words 'Not One Shall Be Forgotten'.

Chapter Seven

'We need more ammunition if we are going to keep fighting this war'

By early October it was clear the Allied advance had slowed and might be approaching a stalemate in the west. Most troubling to Eisenhower was that Antwerp remained unavailable to shipping. The campaign to clear the Schelde estuary leading to the port would not be a simple one. Efforts to capture the south bank of the Schelde in addition to Walcheren island and South Beveland peninsula on the north side of the estuary would involve difficult fighting by Canadian and Polish troops in 21st Army Group, amphibious units and the American 104th Division. The Allies gained control of the estuary in early November and the port at Antwerp would finally begin to receive shipping and supplies at the end of the month.

As a result of the distance to their Normandy bases, American armies experienced shortages of all sorts including ammunition well into the fall. Since priority focused on gasoline, ammunition and food following the breakout from Normandy, items such as warm clothing for the coming colder months and waterproof boots were relegated to a lower transport priority. Considered a calculated risk by Bradley, the consequences became all too clear later in the fall and winter.[1]

Because of supply shortages, particularly of gasoline, Patton's Third Army adopted a policy of aggressive defence, rather than active efforts to advance, that lasted through October. By late September its role had shifted to maintaining front line positions between 6th Army Group to the south and the other two armies in Bradley's 12th Army Group – First and newly-created Ninth – in the north. Vehicles from the Third transported supplies for other armies on the front. The divisions established positions outside Metz and continued with efforts to enlarge bridgeheads over the Moselle. Such crossings had been undertaken south of Metz as early as the second week of September.[2]

Postwar interviews with German military commanders revealed that the Ardennes sector from Aachen south to Trier – essentially along the borders of south-eastern Belgium and Luxembourg – was especially vulnerable in early September. Model signalled that on 8 September only seven or eight battalions held this front of

120 kilometres. Bradley's decision to direct First Army slightly to the north through the Aachen Gap led to entanglement by mid-September in the fortified and reinforced lines around the city.[3] Liddell Hart concluded that efforts to find an easier route to the Rhine resulted in greater difficulties.

The envelopment of Aachen by First Army began in mid-September and these troops encountered concrete casemates and other defensive measures of the West Wall known to the Allies as the Siegfried Line. Divisions pushed into the defensive belt no longer vacant in contrast to late August-early September. As had been the case with the fortified coastal strong points in Normandy, troops soon discovered or rediscovered methods successful in the reduction of such positions.

The 16th Infantry in the 1st Division described combined assaults by infantry and tanks on concrete pill boxes north-west of Aachen. German troops occupied trenches surrounding a fortified position. (Some American officers sleeping inside such a pill box later reported great pressure on the ears when artillery landed nearby, which the 16th thought might explain why Germans dug in outside). After tanks fired on the position, soldiers moved in with hand grenades. Infantry advancing adjacent to tanks constituted the preferred approach, with added support of flame throwers if no enemy tanks were rumbling about the perimeter. In another instance, a pill box camouflaged with earth and surrounded by defended trenches was encountered. Tanks moved up and blew away the camouflage. Machine gun fire kept enemy down and infantry advanced with bazookas.

Some positions sat on high ground within small clearings in woods. Americans found surrounding trees useful in covering their advance. Fortified locations at times contained howitzers and bullet-proof rear doors. However, the rear proved to be the weakest side of the casemate and direct tank fire from the 75mm gun of a Sherman penetrated any door.[4]

Efforts by the 30th and 1st Divisions to move through defences surrounding Aachen met with increasing resistance. Lieutenant Colonel Edmund Driscoll's 1/16th Infantry resisted counter-attacks during 18 September but found Germans remained within grenade range. The battalion reported continual enemy artillery falling on their tired ranks reduced to about 100 men in each company. They expected American artillery would deal with those enemy thought to be from the 9th Panzergrenadier Regiment entrenching nearby. One prisoner of war stated the German companies each held only sixty men.

Reports indicated shortages of high-priority items such as mortar ammunition. Deliveries of 60mm and light 81mm shells stopped for a time in mid-September (the 16th Infantry had 900 of the former on hand) but some heavy 81mm mortar shells were expected in the morning. During the same period the 16th noted it held 150 cans of gas but the reserve dwindled to 56 cans. Clothing concerns remained; the regimental supply officer expected 3,000 pairs of socks in a few days.[5] The socks would be appreciated in the increasing cold of fall on the continent.

Various methods emerged to confuse and confound American attacks – after the Americans had fired red smoke shells to mark positions for airplanes to bomb, the defenders fired blue smoke at the same location in hopes of diverting the planes. In other instances, German artillery placed red smoke on opposing lines to promote bombing by 'friendly' tactical air support. On 2 October a propaganda broadcast played popular music by Duke Ellington, Benny Goodman and Artie Shaw while proclaiming Russia and Britain were benefiting at the expense of American lives. In response to a suggested cessation of firing, mortar crews from the 3/26th Infantry laid barrages on German positions. The broadcast ended.[6]

The German high command attempted to assemble forces sufficient to drive the Americans back from Aachen or at least widen the northern corridor into the city. Most of the time, however, arriving troops deployed piecemeal to halt attacks. American forces continued to encircle the city and moved to subdue defended hills along the northern edge.

The 16th Infantry maintained a line extending east of the city from Eilendorf to Stolberg. This line and that held by the 18th Infantry received sharp counter-attacks from two newly-arrived units: the 116th Panzer Division and the 3rd Panzergrenadier Division. The latter assaulted the 16th lines along a ridge in mid-October, with the attack falling heavily on Company G of Captain Joe Dawson and Company I of Captain Kimball Richmond. The companies and their commanders distinguished themselves inland from Omaha Beach on 6 June.

Attacks launched on the 14th against positions of Companies G and I were driven back by combined efforts of infantry supported by artillery and tactical air, but resumed late evening and into the early hours of 15 October. Enemy infantry overran some Company G fox holes and when reinforced retained control of them through-out the day. Company I was attacked by perhaps a battalion of German infantry from 3rd Panzergrenadier Division supported by tanks that enabled them to occupy a concrete pill box. During the afternoon the 3rd Battalion commander Lieutenant Colonel Charles Horner stated, 'we need more ammunition if we are going to keep fighting this war.'

Late on the 15th Dawson reported that what seemed to be an enemy withdrawal in the afternoon in reality served to create a reserve. Another attack with fresh troops on the left front of the American position was driven back by rifle and machine gun fire. A company from the 26th Infantry moved behind the line to provide support.

Early in the morning of the 16th Dawson conceived a plan to disrupt another anticipated attack. He hoped to move tanks and tank destroyers behind his lines, after which infantry would seek shelter deep in their holes and artillery would lay down a barrage behind German armour along the American front. Should the enemy tanks move back the intensity of the barrage would only increase; if they advanced they would become targets for American armour. Regardless, by late morning it seemed possible the company may withdraw from the hill if the Germans renewed their attacks. By the afternoon, however, Company G reoccupied fox holes overrun the previous day, discovering that eight of ten men believed missing remained in position. The pill box in the Company I sector was also reoccupied that day.

On the evening of the 16th the 2nd Battalion reported to the regiment the men had not eaten a hot meal since the night of the 14th and asked if warm food could be provided on the following day. It must have seemed they deserved it. MacDonald concluded it was not clear if Dawson's plan 'to knock them out or make them fight' succeeded or was even implemented, but the day was saved in part by a company that did not recognize when it was beaten.[7]

The Germans struggled to maintain the northern corridor through which supplies and reinforcements could enter Aachen and civilian refugees flee. Aerial bombardment increased destruction in the city but did little to reduce defensive effectiveness. Fighting within the city from mid-October onwards was undertaken by two battalions from the 26th Infantry of the 1st Division. On 12 October the 3rd Battalion of Lieutenant Colonel John Corley launched into the factory complex and hills at the northern side of the city while the 2nd Battalion of Lieutenant Colonel Derrill Daniel moved westward toward the centre.[8]

Various techniques employed throughout the month to reduce enemy positions included 155mm self-propelled rifles capable of collapsing buildings that withstood the smaller guns of tanks. The threatened use of flame throwers would result in surrender of some locations. In one instance troops sent a street car labelled 'V-3' laden with explosives careening into the city.

Daniel's 2nd Battalion advanced methodically by street, clearing positions house by house. Each platoon moved in concert with a tank or tank destroyer and was covered by machine gun fire. Artillery pounded building after building ahead of the advance. Linkages were maintained with platoons on neighbouring streets to avoid one group advancing too far and becoming isolated. Buildings could not be bypassed since German troops would emerge later to stage rear attacks. Even sewers were cleared and manhole covers sealed.

The 3rd Battalion in the northern part of the city entered Farwick Park. A counterattack on 15 October for a time drove them back but positions were soon restored. The 18th Infantry moved north of Aachen and eventually made contact with elements of the 30th Division, thus closing the northern corridor on the afternoon of the 16th.

Farwick Park and associated buildings including the imposing Hotel Quellenhof were secured and occupied on the 18th. The Lousberg heights fell on the 19th and resistance crumbled that day and into the 20th. As the overall western commander Field Marshal von Rundstedt reminded garrison commander Oberst Gerhard Wilck,

Hitler decreed the city should be defended to the last, but such warnings did little to stave off the inevitable. As the 3rd Battalion prepared to pound his command post inside an air raid shelter with 155mm shells, Oberst Wilck decided further resistance was futile and surrendered the city around midday on 21 October.[9]

Aachen, known by several names during its long history including Aix-la-Chapelle, had Roman origins and was the Carolingian seat of Aquisgranum in the ninth century. Charlemagne was born there and began an association with the Holy Roman Empire lasting into the sixteenth century. Aachen held an honoured place in National Socialist mythology and German nationalism.[10]

By late October the city lay in ruins. The defenders, who at times outnumbered forces deployed to capture the city, delayed the American advance into the Aachen Gap. Nevertheless, the Allies hoped for one more mobile effort before the onset of winter. Troops of First Army passed around and through the city. Those who moved to the east entered the Hürtgen Forest in attempts to seize dams on the River Roer and perhaps cross that river and even move to the Rhine.

A GI stands in the chapel of Rimsburg Castle near the Dutch-German border on 4 October. (*NARA*)

(**Opposite, above**) An aerial view of Aachen on 29 September. The hill in the centre is the Lousberg, known to Americans as Observatory Hill, one of the defended high ground positions occupied by German troops within the northern district of the city. (*NARA*)

(**Above**) Occupation of the interior of Aachen was the responsibility of the 26th Infantry, 1st Division. Moran photographed Company L of the 3rd Battalion advancing past factory buildings on 13 October. (*NARA*)

(**Opposite, below**) Numerous photographs recorded fighting on 15 October within the city. Ellet witnessed a soldier advancing past a burning building. (*NARA*)

(**Above**) A soldier from the 2nd Battalion of the 26th Infantry on the same day. (*NARA*)

(**Opposite, above**) A 2nd Battalion machine gun crew provided fire support as infantry advanced along a street. (*NARA*)

(**Opposite, below**) Ellet stood with the crew of a 57mm anti-tank gun in the city. (*NARA*)

(**Opposite, above**) Company M from the 26th Infantry moved behind a Sherman tank into the city. Each infantry platoon was generally assisted by the gun of a tank or tank destroyer during the slow advance along the streets (MacDonald, *Siegfried Line*, p. 310). *(NARA)*

(**Above**) Members of the 2nd Battalion accepted the surrender of soldiers in Aachen on the same day, 15 October, as photographed by Ellet. *(NARA)*

(**Opposite, below**) Wescott photographed Private First Class Hoyle Lougherty beside the warning 'Feind hört mit!' or 'the enemy may be listening'. *(NARA)*

(**Opposite, above**) Civilians had been urged to evacuate the town by the Germans and some of those who remained left on the 15th. These citizens piled a few belongings on a cart. (*NARA*)

(**Above**) Ellet encountered civilians with baggage on an Aachen street the same day. (*NARA*)

(**Opposite, below**) Wescott met a stalwart citizen two days later with an impressive mustache who with his goal had no intention of leaving. (*NARA*)

The German commander Oberst (Colonel) Gerhard Wilck finally agreed to surrender the city when ammunition supplies were virtually exhausted and further resistance was futile. An American jeep transported the dejected garrison commander, his staff and their blankets and baggage on 21 October. (NARA)

Zwick recorded the devastation of a district in Aachen that included a cruciform church without its dome in an aerial view on 24 October. (NARA)

195612-S

The Aachen Münster, also termed Charlemagne Cathedral, in a central district in the city, photographed by Moran on the 24th. (*NARA*)

195848

Augustins photographed damage to Saint Joseph's church in Aachen on 27 October. (*NARA*)

Artillery fire devastated much of the city, including Einbahnstrasse, photographed by Wescott on the same day, the 27th. *(NARA)*

Katy photographed an American casualty wrapped in a blanket in preparation for retrieval by a Graves Registration unit on 23 October. The location near Bruyères in the Alsace region of eastern France indicated the soldier was a member of Seventh Army near Strasbourg. *(NARA)*

A former German trench close to the town of Monschau in the Ardennes was occupied on 25 October by Corporal Amons and Private First Class Gunnich from First Army. (*NARA*)

195855-S

Privates Carrington and Gross fire from a trench along a dyke probably in Holland on 1 November. *(NARA)*

Chapter Eight

'The men in town are going to take a beating'

Cold weather arrived in north-west Europe by late September of 1944. Due to limitations in transport capacity, priority in late summer and early fall focused on fuel, ammunition and rations. Movement of warm clothing and footgear was a secondary priority. Now the American armies would begin to suffer from those decisions. Despite improvements in transportation compared with October, the supply problem occasioned by the continued inability to use the port of Antwerp into November weighed heavily on offensive operations all along the front.

Mud was an increasing problem in the fall. Standing in trenches or fox holes filled with near-freezing mud and water inevitably led to trench foot, sometimes resulting in gangrene and amputations. From October 1944 to April 1945 more than 46,000 American soldiers entered hospitals due to trench foot, representing 9 per cent of casualties during the campaign.[1]

The standard leather combat shoes or boots were not waterproof. Men were encouraged to use foot powder after drying their feet and to regularly change to dry socks, but perpetual wetness rendered such techniques of limited value. Soldiers would, according to Mauldin, stumble or crawl to aid stations for such relief as could be provided. Unless they lost use of their feet, however, they would soon be sent back to the line.[2]

The First Army launched a concerted assault east of Aachen through the densely wooded and irregular terrain of the Hürtgen Forest. Successive divisions attempted to advance with limited success and high numbers of casualties. The 9th Division entered in September, moved to seize Schmidt in October, and was replaced by the 28th Division in this task. The 28th lasted in the forest until the middle of November. The 1st Division near Aachen just to the west advanced on that flank into the forest in the latter part of November. Efforts were made by the 4th, 8th and 83rd Divisions, the 2nd Ranger Battalion and the 5th Armoured Division. In excess of 25 per cent of these troops became casualties. They were felled either by bullets, shell fragments and mines or by 'non-battle' causes such as trench foot, diarrhoea, exposure and combat fatigue.[3]

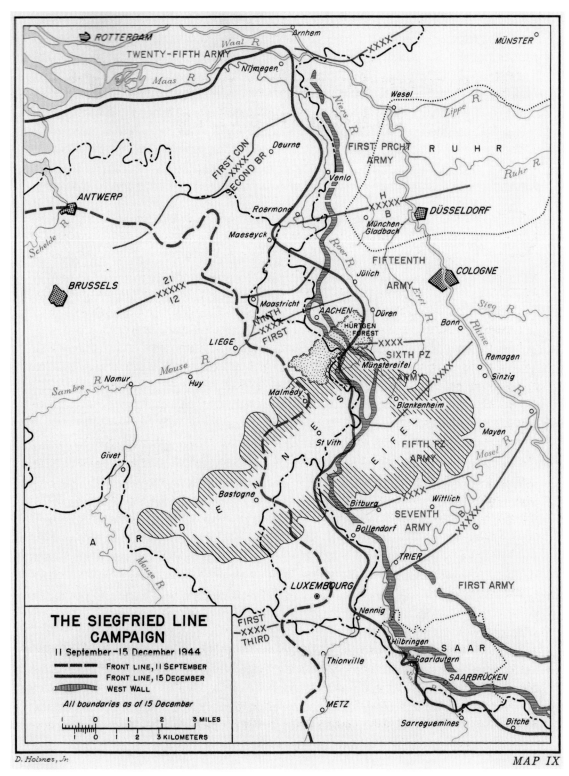

THE SIEGFRIED LINE
CAMPAIGN
11 September – 15 December 1944

FRONT LINE, 11 SEPTEMBER
FRONT LINE, 15 DECEMBER
WEST WALL

All boundaries as of 15 December

3 MILES

3 KILOMETERS

D. Holmes, Jr.

MAP IX

From MacDonald, *The Siegfried Line Campaign.*

As the 28th Division entered the Hürtgen Forest in early November men who possessed overshoes in the muddy conditions numbered only ten to fifteen on average per infantry company.[4] The division sought to occupy Schmidt beyond Vossenack in the south-eastern corner of the forest. Narrow trackways and woodland paths that passed for roads in the forest became so muddy that operations were seriously impeded. The result as described by Charles MacDonald was among the most costly battles by an American division in the Second World War.[5]

The 3rd Battalion of the 112th Infantry moved along such a route – the Kall River trail – to capture Schmidt on 3 November despite tanks stuck on the narrow trail preventing passage of other vehicles. The battalion could not hold the village when subjected to a sustained counter-attack the following day. Small groups of men fell back to Kommerscheidt in panic and varying states of confusion, groups reluctant to respond to orders from officers and other men from the supporting 1st Battalion.[6]

The depleted force in Kommerscheidt finally withdrew into woods to the north on 7 November following attacks by infantry from the 89th Division and tanks from the 16th Panzer Regiment, 116th Panzer Division, the unit that participated in efforts to relieve Aachen in mid-October. The following day remnants of the 112th Infantry from Kommerscheidt withdrew across the Kall and ascended the trail to occupy an upland ridge. During the same period the 2nd Battalion of the 112th withdrew from the eastern end of Vossenack on the 6th before driving out infantry from the two panzergrenadier regiments in 116th Panzer Division to regain control of the village on the 7th. The 2nd Battalion was assisted by the 146th Engineer Battalion fighting as infantry on that day.[7]

Divisions repeatedly found movement difficult and on occasion impossible in the forest. One that struggled as much as any was the 8th Division. Trench foot and combat fatigue in the 121st Infantry Regiment affected both replacements and more seasoned soldiers. Severe cases were evacuated, while others retired to the rear for rest and warm food. Some men simply refused to remain in the line. Master Sergeant Willard Bryan in the regiment noted older men particularly suffered from the weather and if possible were withdrawn and assigned administrative duties to minimize alternative outcomes of court-martial or mental collapse.[8]

The Hürtgen Forest was simply awful and almost nothing was gained to compensate for the losses in killed, wounded and suffering of all who experienced repeated attempts to break through to the River Roer. Americans and Germans were mystified at efforts to advance through closed forested landscapes limiting use of armour, terrain that negated Allied air superiority employed to great effect during the breakout from Normandy to the German border.

Enemy mortars and artillery rained down and troops confronted pill boxes mounting machine guns that despite limited fields of fire were difficult to see in the forest. 'Tree bursts' or explosions of mortar and artillery rounds at the tops of trees were common; as Fussell reasoned, what else would one expect in a forest. Rather than dispersing shrapnel horizontally that often could be avoided in fox holes, tree bursts resulted in vertical descent of shrapnel from which holes offered no protection unless covered with logs.[9] An attack in mid-November by the 2nd Battalion of the 26th Infantry encountered just this problem as they moved forward north-east of Aachen. They in addition noted the German tendency for two-man fox holes to withhold fire during the initial advance until following troops came within range.[10]

When the 1st Division emerged along the eastern edge of the forest the 2/26th Infantry became embroiled in a tragic attack on Merode. Companies E and F entered the town on 29 November but German forces counter-attacked. By evening of the 29th radio contact ceased after receipt of a Company F message indicating sustained firing from enemy infantry and tanks. Just after midnight early on 30 November, the regimental commander Colonel John Seitz sent a dispirited message to division headquarters:

> There is one or two tanks and some infantry in town. Part of 'E' and 'F' Co. is in there. We haven't communication with them nor does White 6 [2nd Battalion commander Lieutenant Colonel Derrill Daniel] who is with 'G' Co. outside in the woods. This is probably as tight a position as we have been in since the operation began. I am afraid the men in town are going to take a beating, but there is nothing we can do about it. Our casualties were heavy today and still coming in.

Efforts at relief on the 30th proved unsuccessful. Infantry could not move forward in the face of enemy fire from tanks, artillery and small arms. Vehicles mired during earlier attempts blocked subsequent movement by supporting tanks on the muddy road leading to the slope on which Merode stood. Continued enemy fire on the near edge of town raised hopes that some men had held out; supporting American artillery pounded the far edge. A few troops that had not entered with the companies straggled in and a prisoner questioned in the evening confirmed the Germans had closed in from woods both above and below the town.[11]

On the morning of 1 December, infantry attempted twice to advance into the town but mortar, artillery and small arms fire halted both efforts. By the afternoon, the regiment decided the two companies and supporting heavy weapons platoons – much of the 2nd Battalion that in October fought into the centre of Aachen – must be considered lost in Merode.[12]

* * *

The 1st Division listed a total of 3,993 battle casualties, including 641 within a regiment attached from the 9th Division, in the Hürtgen Forest. The 26th Infantry alone lost 1,479, the highest among the division's regiments. In addition, men were absent due to non-battle causes.

The 28th Division suffered more casualties – 5,684 in November – than any other unit in the forest. The 112th Infantry sustained 2,093 losses during the month including 232 captured and 431 missing. Non-battle causes accounted for 544 or 26 per cent of the overall losses. MacDonald observed that many successes from Normandy onwards stemmed from gambles, but the attack on Schmidt was a gamble that failed.

The 110th Infantry in the same division offers a sobering perspective from the fall of 1944. During October the regiment listed 208 battle casualties (killed, wounded and missing) compared with 316 non-battle losses (sickness and combat fatigue). The latter represented 60 per cent of the unit's losses during the month, a reflection of deteriorating weather conditions. During November fighting in the Hürtgen Forest, battle casualties increased to 1,204 and non-battle losses to 890, 42.5 per cent of the monthly total. While the overall percentage was lower, the non-battle numerical increase reflected both the worsening weather and the savage fighting.[13]

Charles MacDonald who wrote the official Army historical account found it difficult to justify the effort beyond losses sustained by the enemy and the apparent danger of leaving an unconquered forested area behind advancing lines without sufficient reserves. Subsequent historians Russell Weigley and Stephen Ambrose found it impossible to explain much less justify the debacle.

James Gavin and Paul Fussell felt repeated attacks through such terrain reflected the worst elements of 'chateau generalship' for which the First World War was infamous. It appeared to both the plans were drawn up from maps rather than on-site terrain assessments. Gavin had a chance to study the battlefield in February 1945 in advance of 82nd Airborne's movement down the Kall River trail from Vossenack to Schmidt. Vehicles remained abandoned on the trail and bodies, both Americans from the 28th Division and German defenders, lay unburied and exposed by the melting snow.

Gavin believed the proper route of attack should have followed the ridge northeast from Lammersdorf into Schmidt. The ridge with a paved road and a mixture of woods and open fields suitable for tank manoeuvre seemed far superior to moving down a slope into a river gorge and then up the slope on the opposite side along a narrow and unstable trail. After discussions with V Corps staff, Gavin decided such a question was not appreciated following the Hürtgen disaster.[14]

* * *

By early December the Allied armies along the Western Front, despite optimism resulting from a rapid advance across France in late August and early September, did not cross the River Rhine and only reached the German border at a few places.

A continuous line was maintained from the Schelde estuary near Antwerp across Holland and Belgium along or near the German border and through the French provinces of Lorraine and Alsace to the border with neutral Switzerland. The Third Army achieved a linkage with the 6th Army Group from the Mediterranean in September.

In early November offensive movements were resumed by Third Army with hopes of driving through the Siegfried Line and beyond the Rhine to the Mainz–Frankfurt area. As First Army discovered to the north, German defences had stiffened along the front. The city of Metz on the Moselle finally surrendered on 20 November although some surrounding forts held out into December.

The 4th Armoured Division reached the River Saar on 25 November and in conjunction with the 26th Division approached Saar-Union that was occupied on 4 December. Both divisions approached Sarreguemines near the Saar industrial region during the next week. The 4th Armoured paused to refit and regroup. The division resumed its push on 17 December; the next day the 87th Division that replaced the 26th Division on the line was a few miles inside the German border moving towards Saarbrücken. That same day 4th Armoured pulled out to begin a northward advance to Luxembourg against the German offensive.[15]

* * *

Gavin enjoyed Thanksgiving dinner in Reims then journeyed to London. He returned to the camp in Sissone to learn that 82nd troops misbehaved to such an extent in Reims the local section commander banned them from the town. Gavin restored a reduced number of visits under an increased presence of a special guard from the regiments. He concluded three situations were responsible: 'There is no way to get a girl of easy virtue, all houses are off limits and guarded, food cannot be bought in town anywhere, champagne can be bought by the bottle anywhere anytime.'[16]

During December the troops settled into camp life and resumed training. Some enjoyed passes to Paris and all were glad to be out of the field. Apparently troops on leave were behaving themselves. Gavin learned someone in Paris praised the 'alert' appearance of the 82nd soldiers in Paris; an observer responded of course they were alert since 'you are looking at the survivors'. A particular emphasis was placed on granting leaves after the 101st Airborne chief of staff committed suicide. It will be recalled the chief of staff survived his jump from a flaming transport plane during Market Garden.

In October Gavin met the journalist Martha Gelhorn, soon to become the third ex-wife of Ernest Hemingway. He later commented that she wrote a 'grand' article for *Collier's Magazine* and invited her to a 'Prop Blast' scheduled for 19 December.[17] Events in the Ardennes led to a cancellation of the dance.

The 1st Division moved in early December south-west into Belgium. The division spent time resting and incorporating new soldiers into its ranks. The 26th Infantry for example needed replacements for virtually all personnel in the ill-fated Companies E and F. The position of the division in eastern Belgium proved fortuitous in mid-December.

When the 28th Division sustained many casualties in the south-east corner of the forest by mid-November, the infantry regiments, artillery and associated divisional troops moved south into Luxembourg. The sector was a quiet one and the intention was to provide an opportunity for the division to rest and incorporate yet more replacements into its ranks. By mid-December, the 28th Division occupied positions directly in the path of the German offensive through the Ardennes.

Goodman photographed members of Company E 110th Infantry in the 28th Division on 2 November near Vossenack in the Hürtgen Forest. These men paraded along the Champs-Élysées in Paris slightly more than two months earlier. (NARA)

232855

Eisenhower visited the commander of VIII Corps Troy Middleton in Saint-Vith, Belgium, on 9 November. The photographer Moore was present to record the pair in conversation. *(NARA)*

(**Opposite, above**) Tank destroyers moving along a muddy and narrow trail in the rugged terrain of the Hürtgen Forest on 8 November. The 1st Battalion with remnants of 3rd Battalion 112th Infantry withdrew from woods outside of Kommerscheidt back across the River Kall that day and these tank destroyers may have supported the movement. (*NARA*)

(**Opposite, below**) Three soldiers from Company I in 8th Infantry of the 4th Division in the forest on 18 November: Private First Class Maurice Berson and Staff Sergeants Bernard Spurr and Harold Glessler. (*NARA*)

(**Above**) Soldiers from the same Company I wounded on the 18th in the effort to reach Düren beyond the forest. (*NARA*)

Moran photographed Company I medics assisting a wounded soldier in the forest on the same day, 18 November. (*NARA*)

Mud was an overwhelming challenge contributing to the misery of the Hürtgen Forest. Corrado observed attempts to extract a medical evacuation jeep on 27 November. (*NARA*)

One unit possessed a mascot named 'Sergeant Sabu' after a possible GI expression 'Situation all but unrecognizable'. The sergeant, apparently adept at smelling buried mines, was photographed on 3 December. *(NARA)*

(**Above**) A German Panther with crew destroyed by Seventh Army near Schalbach, France, south-east of Sarreguemines, photographed on 3 December. (*NARA*)

(**Opposite**) Staff Sergeant Joseph Verhagen spots gunfire from the 709th Field Artillery Battalion in support of infantry from the 8th Division near the Hürtgen Forest. Crompton photographed the scene on 4 December. (*NARA*)

(**Opposite**) Stephen Longstreth from Carnegie, Pennsylvania, and Company I in 121st Infantry of the 8th Division emerged to eat his first hot meal following fifteen days near Hürtgen. Weart recorded the meal on 5 December. Longstreth was wearing rubber overshoes or galoshes. The long winter coat was soon abandoned by many infantry soldiers. Long wool coats restricted movement and became heavy when wet. (*NARA*)

(**Above**) A soldier from Battery B 997 Field Artillery Battalion managed a smile despite the mud encasing his tracked howitzer. Poinsett must have been a persuasive photographer, at least on 7 December. (*NARA*)

(**Left**) Sergeant John Parks was photographed by Orntiz on 10 December after many days in his tank on the line. Parks, aged 24, was killed shortly afterwards (Kennett, *G.I.*, between pp. 164 and 165). (*NARA*)

A group of Germans near Jüngersdorf just beyond the Hürtgen Forest on 12 December. These men were prisoners of Company I in 39th Infantry of the 9th Division. (NARA)

The photographer English witnessed mine clearance on a slope in the Hürtgen Forest on 14 December. Artillery fire shattered the upper portions of trees in the forest. These tree bursts rained shrapnel and wood splinters down from which uncovered fox holes offered little protection. (NARA)

Clancy witnessed 9th Infantry soldiers sheltering in a trench from artillery fire in the Krinkelter Woods on the same day, 14 December. (NARA)

Image Credits

NB: Page numbers are in **bold**. Any images not credited are from the author's collection.

Chapter One: An Army in France
9 NARA 111-SC-270804; **10** NARA 111-SC-192223; **11** (top) NARA 111-SC-209308, (bottom) NARA 111-SC-192250; **12** NARA 111-SC-192078; **13** (top) NARA 111-SC-192765, (bottom) NARA 111-SC-192516; **14** (top) NARA 111-SC-192694, (bottom) NARA 111-SC-332085; **15** NARA 111-SC-325642; **16** (top) NARA 111-SC-210076, (bottom) NARA 111-SC-333948; **17** NARA 111-SC-192471; **18** (top) NARA 111-SC-192372, (bottom) NARA 111-SC-192455; **19** NARA 111-SC-417623; **20** (top) NARA 111-SC-192554, (bottom) NARA 111-SC-192662; **21** NARA 111-SC-192753; **22** NARA 111-SC-192509.

Chapter Two: Inferno in Normandy
30 IWM C 4571; **31** (top) NARA 111-SC-344758, (bottom) NARA 111-SC-192984; **32** (top) NARA 111-SC-192968, (bottom) NARA 111-SC-193111; **33** NARA 111-SC-377953; **34** (top) NARA 111-SC-193093, (bottom) Mémorial de Montormel and Library and Archives Canada a111565; **35** Mémorial de Montormel; **36** (top) NARA 111-SC-193081, (bottom) NARA 111-SC-192738; **37** NARA 111-SC-193116; **38** NARA 111-SC-332120 ; **39** (top) NARA 111-SC-354638 (bottom) NARA 111-SC-401630; **40** (top) NARA 111-SC-364274, (bottom) NARA 111-SC-193312; **41** NARA 111-SC-193117; **42** (top) NARA 111-SC-193118, (bottom) NARA 111-SC-192922; **43** (top) IWM HU 31069 (bottom) NARA 111-SC-192927.

Chapter Three: 'The day the war should have ended'
52 NARA 111-SC-192467; **53** NARA 111-SC-192468; **54** (top) NARA 111-SC-192626, (bottom) NARA 111-SC-192991; **55** NARA 111-SC-192967 ; **56** NARA 111-SC-443064; **57** (top) NARA 111-SC-364273, (bottom) NARA 111-SC-193339; **58** (top) ARA 111-SC-193340, (bottom) NARA 111-SC-193233; **59** NARA 111-SC-193235; **60** (top) NARA 111-SC-193344, (bottom) NARA 111-SC-193338; **61** NARA 111-SC-193236; **62** NARA 111-SC-192998; **63** NARA 111-SC-193007; **64** (top) NARA 111-SC-192999, bottom NARA 111-SC-193372; **65** NARA 111-SC-193008; **66** NARA 111-SC-193009; **67** (top) NARA 111-SC-193010, (bottom) NARA 111-SC-193251; **68** (top) NARA 111-SC-192993, (bottom) NARA 111-SC-193328; **69** NARA 111-SC-193345; **70** (top) NARA 111-SC-193334, (bottom) NARA 111-SC-193330; **71** NARA 111-SC-193373; **72** (top) NARA 111-SC-193084, (bottom) NARA 111-SC-193085; **73** NARA 111-SC-193200; **74** (top) NARA 111-SC-210069, (bottom) NARA 111-SC-193197.

Chapter Four: To the Border
80 (top) NARA 111-SC-193349, (bottom) NARA 111-SC-210053; **81** NARA 111-SC-192193; **82** NARA 111-SC-193835; **83** (top) NARA 111-SC-199844, (bottom) NARA 111-SC-193905; **84** (top) NARA 111-SC-194135, (bottom) NARA 111-SC-193923; **85** NARA 111-SC-194840; **86** (top) NARA 111-SC-210060, (bottom) NARA 111-SC-227590.

Chapter Five: 'When in doubt, lash out'
98 NARA 111-SC-232812; **99** (top) NARA 111-SC-377588, (bottom) NARA 111-SC-213277; **100** NARA 111-SC-232810; **101** (top) NARA 111-SC-254001, (bottom) NARA 111-SC-377589;

102 (top) NARA 111-SC-195369, (bottom) NARA 111-SC-194661; **103** NARA 111-SC-210047; **104** NARA 111-SC-347398; **105** (top) NARA 111-SC-354702, (bottom) NARA 111-SC-354703; **106** NARA 111-SC-354700; **107** (top) NARA 111-SC-354701; **109** NARA 111-SC-210051; **110** NARA 111-SC-210052; **111** (top) NARA 111-SC-195100, (bottom) NARA 111-SC-194180; **112** NARA 111-SC-195096; **113** (top) NARA 111-SC-195095, (bottom) NARA 111-SC-377616; **115** (bottom left) NARA 111-SC-313643, (bottom right) NARA 111-SC-313710; **116** NARA 111-SC-195097; **117** (top) NARA 111-SC-195099; **119** NARA 111-SC-194590; **120** NARA 111-SC-194337; **121** (top) NARA 111-SC-377590, (bottom) NARA 111-SC-194591; **122** NARA 111-SC-194409; **123** (top) NARA 111-SC-194335, (bottom) NARA 111-SC-194592.

Chapter Six: 'Not one shall be forgotten'
133 (top) NARA 111-SC-377615; **136** (bottom) IWM BU 1103; **138** (top) NARA 111-SC-194408; **139** NARA 111-SC-194336; **140** (top right) NARA 111-SC-313779, (bottom) NARA 111-SC-194587; **141** NARA 111-SC-194445; **142** (top) NARA 111-SC-194583, (bottom) NARA 111-SC-194582; **143** (top) NARA 111-SC-194584, (bottom) NARA 111-SC-194796; **144** (top) NARA 111-SC-194797, (bottom) NARA 111-SC-195211; **145** NARA 111-SC-194795; **146** (top) NARA 111-SC-195212, (bottom) NARA 111-SC-195213; **148** NARA 111-SC-194410; **149** (top) NARA 111-SC-195817, (bottom) NARA 111-SC-195925; **150** NARA 111-SC-254005; **151** (top) NARA 111-SC-194567, (bottom) NARA 111-SC- 194681; **152** NARA 111-SC-194568; **153** (bottom) NARA 111-SC-201538; **154** NARA 111-SC-301256; **155** (top) NARA 111-SC-286359, (bottom) NARA 111-SC-286334; **156** (top) NARA 111-SC-483375.

Chapter Seven: 'We need more ammunition . . .'
163 NARA 111-SC-195156; **164** (top) NARA 111-SC-195162, (bottom) NARA 111-SC-332019; **165** NARA 111-SC-195646; **166** NARA 111-SC-195472; **167** (top) NARA 111-SC-195463, (bottom) NARA 111-SC-195469; **168** (top) NARA 111-SC-195638, (bottom) NARA 111-SC-195639; **169** NARA 111-SC-195473; **170** (top) NARA 111-SC-195255, (bottom) NARA 111-SC-195640; **171** NARA 111-SC-195470; **172** (top) NARA 111-SC-195923, (bottom) NARA 111-SC-195612; **173** NARA 111-SC-332962; **174** NARA 111-SC-195848; **175** (top) NARA 111-SC-195849; (bottom) NARA 111-SC-195852; **176** NARA 111-SC-195853; **177** NARA 111-SC-195855.

Chapter Eight: 'The men in town are going to take a beating'
184 NARA 111-SC-334992; **185** NARA 111-SC-232855; **186** (top) NARA 111-SC-196618, (bottom) NARA 111-SC-196619; **187** NARA 111-SC-196620; **188** (top) NARA 111-SC-198841, (bottom) NARA 111-SC-353391; **189** NARA 111-SC-196948; **190** NARA 111-SC-196952; **191** NARA 111-SC-330433; **192** NARA 111-SC-196947; **193** (top) NARA 111-SC-353394; (bottom) NARA 111-SC-197284; **194** NARA 111-SC-197307; **195** (top) NARA 111-SC-341538, (bottom) NARA 111-SC-197304.

Notes

Chapter One: An Army in France

1. Patton, *War As I Knew It*, 88.
2. Bennett, *Ultra in the West*, 111.
3. 120th Infantry A/A Report Battle of Mortain, 5–6.
4. Ibid, 8–12.
5. Third Army Campaign of France, 1–5.
6. Third Army Campaign of France, 8.

Chapter Two: Inferno in Normandy

1. Bradley, *A Soldier's Story*, 376, 377; Patton, *War As I Knew It*, 104.
2. Ibid, 377–9.
3. Blumenson, *Breakout and Pursuit*, 508.
4. Wilmot, *Struggle for Europe*, 417, 424–5; Meyer, *12th SS Panzer* II, 25–6, 69; Florentin, *Battle of Falaise Gap*, 157.
5. Florentin, 177; Meyer, 80–1.
6. Blumenson, 532.
7. Blumenson, 529–30, 534; Florentin, 181, 187–8, 218–9.
8. Florentin, 149, 223–4; Keegan, *Six Armies*, 275.
9. Blumenson, 544; Florentin, 237; Keegan, 274, 277–8.
10. Florentin, 261.
11. Blumenson, 538, 544.
12. Florentin, 274.
13. Blumenson, 544–8.
14. Blumenson, 553.
15. Florentin, 253.
16. Blumenson, 553.
17. Meyer, 109.
18. Florentin, 276.
19. Florentin, 277–8.
20. Florentin, 278; Keegan, 282.
21. Blumenson, 554–8.
22. Blumenson, 558.
23. Eisenhower, *Crusade in Europe*, 279.
24. Fussell, *The Boys' Crusade*, 62, 64; Florentin, *passim*.
25. de Guingand, *Operation Victory*, 407; Wilmot, 417.
26. Keegan, 261; Hastings, *Overlord*, 314–5.

Chapter Three: 'The day the war should have ended'

1. Keegan, 289–91.
2. Blumenson, *Breakout and Pursuit*, 590–7.

3. Collins and Lapierre, *Is Paris Burning?*, 171–3.
4. Patton, *War As I Knew It*, 105.
5. Blumenson, 598–602; Collins and Lapierre, 152, 217.
6. Collins and Lapierre, 193–4, 199–200.
7. Keegan, 340.
8. Blumenson, 608.
9. Collins and Lapierre, 206–8.
10. Blumenson, 610–1; Collins and Lapierre, 228–9.
11. Blumenson, 613; Collins and Lapierre, 239.
12. Collins and Lapierre, 229, 238, 240.
13. Bradley, *A Soldier's Story*, 392.
14. Blumenson, 614–5; Collins and Lapierre, 254–5; Keegan, 308.
15. Graham Kelsey, personal communication.
16. Collins and Lapierre, 218; Blumenson, 615.
17. Collins and Lapierre, 290; Keegan, 310.
18. Keegan, 310–1.
19. Collins and Lapierre, between 256–7.
20. Collins and Lapierre, *Is Paris Burning?*, 288–92; Keegan, *Six Armies*, 311.
21. Hemingway, 'A Room on the Garden Side'.

Chapter Four: To the Border
1. Horrocks, *Corps Commander*, 71–81.
2. Third Army Campaign of France, 10–12.; Cole, *Lorraine Campaign*, maps IX and X.
3. Richardson and Allan, *Subsistence*, 46.
4. Mauldin, *Up Front*, 171–2.
5. Montgomery, *Memoirs*, map 42.
6. Keegan, 315.
7. Patton, *War As I Knew It*, 115–6.
8. Ryan, *A Bridge Too Far*, 85–8.
9. Bennett, *Ultra in the West*, 145–55.
10. Horrocks, *Corps Commander*, 81.
11. Liddell Hart, *History of the Second World War*, 563–7.
12. Horrocks, 62–3, 83.
13. de Guingand, *Operation Victory*, 410–4.

Chapter Five: 'When in doubt, lash out'
1. Gavin diary, 14 September 1944.
2. Horrocks, 96–100.
3. 2nd Bn Irish Guards War Diary, 17 September 1944.
4. FitzGerald, *Irish Guards*, 489–95.
5. 2nd Bn Irish Guards War Diary, 18 September 1944.
6. 506th Journal, 17 September 1944.
7. Marshall and Westover, 502nd at Best, 12–21.
8. Marshall and Westover, 502–1 at St Oedenrode, 11–23.
9. Marshall and Westover, 502nd at Best, 27–39.
10. Marshall and Westover, 1st Bn 501st.
11. Ambrose, *Band of Brothers*, 137.

12. Gavin, *On to Berlin*, 151; 82nd Combat Interviews (C.I.) Gavin letter to Captain Westover, 25 July 1945.
13. Thuring and Heij, *Verdwenen Kerkhoven*; C. I. Company A 504th.
14. Gavin, 157–9; C. I. 2nd Bn 504th. The 504th did not participate in the Normandy invasion since it fought earlier in 1944 at Anzio.
15. Combat Interview letter Lieutenant Colonel Lindquist, 14 September 1945.
16. 505th A/A Report, 5; Gavin, 168.
17. Thuring and Heij, *Verdwenen Kerkhoven*; Gavin, 173
18. 505th A/A Report, 7; Gavin, 175–7
19. C.I. 3rd Bn 504th, 4–6.
20. 2nd Bn Irish Guards War Diary, 20 September 1944.
21. C.I. 3rd Bn 504th, 7, 9.
22. Ryan, *A Bridge Too Far*, 463.
23. 504th A/A Report, 3; C.I. Company G 504th, 17.
24. C.I. 3rd Bn 504th, 17; Thuring and Heij, *Verdwenen Kerkhoven*.
25. C.I. 1st Bn and Company B 504th.
26. Thuring and Heij, *Verdwenen Kerkhoven*; Captain Rosen was a recent parachute school graduate (Gavin diary, 30 July 1944).
27. Horrocks, *Corps Commander*, 116–7.
28. 3rd Bn Irish Guards War Diary, 20 September 1944.

Chapter Six: 'Not one shall be forgotten'

1. 1st British Airborne A/A Report, 5–6.
2. 1st British Airborne A/A Report, 8–9; Ellis, *Victory in the West Vol. II*, 46–7.
3. 1st British Airborne War Diary, 17–19 September 1944; on 19th '1325 Report from RA that remains of 2 and 3 Para Bns with HQ 1 Para Bde were established at NORTH end of br 7476 and that Lt. Col. FROST, OC 2 Para Bn was in comd.'
4. 504th and 505th Journals, 18 September 1944.
5. 1st British Airborne A/A Report, 16–7; Ellis, *Victory in the West Vol. II*, 48–9.
6. 2nd Bn Irish Guards War Diary, 20 September 1944.
7. Horrocks, 117; Gavin, *On to Berlin*, 181–2.
8. 1st British Airborne War Diary, 21 September 1944 '0115 Phantom received message Guards Armoured Div to go flat out at first light for brs at ARNHEM …'
9. FitzGerald, *Irish Guards*, 511–2; Ryan, *A Bridge Too Far*, 509.
10. 1st British Airborne A/A Report, 25; Ryan, 535–7, 543.
11. 1st British Airborne A/A Report, 25; Ryan, 568–71.
12. Ellis, *Victory the West Vol. II*, 37, 42; 506th Unit Journal, 19 and 22–23 September 1944; Ryan, 534.
13. Ellis, *Vol. II*, 43–4.
14. 506th Journal, 24 September 1944; Ryan, 564, 568; Urquhart, *Arnhem*, 160, 168–70, 178, 181–2.
15. Ellis, *Vol. II*, 55.
16. Urquhart, 117–9; Horrocks, 120–1.
17. Ryan, 502.
18. Urquhart, 146.
19. Montgomery, *Memoirs*, 267.
20. Ryan, 89, quoting Eisenhower comment to Stephen Ambrose.
21. Gavin diary, 8 October 1944. These remarks may reflect the dark tone of the entry occasioned by receipt of General Ridgway's letter over a perceived slight during the actions around Nijmegen.

22. Combat Interview letter to Captain Westover, 25 July 1945.
23. MacDonald, *Siegfried Line*, 199–200. Charles MacDonald led an infantry company in the 2nd Division but despite this traditional orientation thought the airborne Market Garden plan was sound if perhaps overambitious.
24. Ambrose, *Band of Brothers*, 141.
25. MacDonald, *Siegfried Line*, 206.
26. 326th Airborne Medical Company A/A Report Holland Mission.
27. 101st 'Alleged Looting', 8 November 1944.
28. Gavin diary, 1 and 10 November 1944.
29. Gavin diary, 1 November 1944.
30. Gavin diary, 22 March 1945.
31. Gavin diary, 13 November 1944.

Chapter Seven: 'We need more ammunition if we are going to keep fighting this war'
1. Bradley, *A Soldier's Story*, 445.
2. Third Army Campaign of France, 11; MacDonald, 'River Crossing at Arnaville'.
3. Wilmot, *Struggle for Europe*, 496–7; Liddell Hart, *History of the Second World War*, 560.
4. 16th Journal, 18 September 1944.
5. 16th Journal, 18 and 19 September 1944.
6. 26th A/A Report October 1944.
7. 16th Journal, 15–16 October 1944; MacDonald, *Siegfried Line*, 293. MacDonald listed Joe Dawson as a lieutenant colonel in command of the 2nd Battalion; the journal referred to him as captain and indicated he remained in command of Company G.
8. MacDonald, *Siegfried Line*, 309–10.
9. MacDonald, 306, 310–16; 26th A/A Report October 1944.
10. MacDonald, *Siegfried Line*, 281.

Chapter Eight: 'The men in town are going to take a beating'
1. Richardson and Allan, *Outfitting the Soldier*, 85; Fussell, *The Boys' Crusade*, 89.
2. Mauldin, *Up Front*, 35–7.
3. Fussell, 85–6.
4. MacDonald, *Siegfried Line*, 386–7.
5. MacDonald, 'Objective: Schmidt', 414–5.
6. MacDonald, 'Objective: Schmidt', 306.
7. MacDonald, 'Objective: Schmidt', 390–1, 402–6.
8. MacDonald, *Siegfried Line*, 455–6.
9. Fussell, 86.
10. 26th A/A Report November 1944, 2.
11. 26th A/A Report November 1944, 5; 26th Journal, 30 November 1944.
12. 26th A/A Report December 1944, 1.
13. MacDonald, *Siegfried Line*, 492–3, MacDonald, 'Objective: Schmidt', 415–6; 110th A/A Reports October and November 1944.
14. Gavin, *On to Berlin*, 261–5; Fussell, *The Boys' Crusade*, 85–91.
15. Third Army Moselle, Metz and Saar Campaign.
16. Gavin diary, 28 November 1944.
17. Gavin diary, 14 December 1944.

References

Army unit records, National Archives Record Group 407

Third US Army summary Campaign of France, 1 August–24 September 1944.

Third US Army summary Moselle, Metz and Saar Campaign, 25 September–18 December 1944.

Combat Interviews 82nd Airborne Division for Holland 1944, National Archives, RG 407:

   Letter: Captain John Westover Office of Theatre Historian to Chief of Staff 82nd Airborne Division, 17 July 1945.

   Letter: Major General James Gavin to Captain John Westover, 25 July 1945 with enclosures.

   Letter: Colonel Roy Lindquist in response to questions, 14 September 1945.

   82nd Airborne Division summary.

   1st Battalion, 504th Parachute Infantry.

   Company A, 1st Battalion, 504th Parachute Infantry.

   Company B, 1st Battalion, 504th Parachute Infantry.

   Major Edward N. Wellems, CO 2nd Battalion, 504th Parachute Infantry.

   3rd Battalion, 504th Parachute Infantry.

   Company G, 3rd Battalion, 504th Regiment by Major O'Sullivan.

101st Airborne Division 'Alleged Looting by United States Troops' in Holland, 8 November 1944.

16th Infantry After Action or A/A Report, September and October 1944.

History 16th CT Breach of the Siegfried Line Germany, 11–23 September 1944.

16th Infantry Unit Journal, September and October 1944.

26th Infantry A/A Report, September–December 1944 and Unit Journal, November 1944.

110th Infantry A/A Report, August–November 1944.

110th Infantry Unit Journal, November 1944.

120th Infantry A/A Report, August 1944 Battle of Mortain.

326th Airborne Medical Company A/A Report on Holland Mission by Major William Barfield.

504th Parachute Infantry A/A Report on Holland by Private First Class David Whittier.

504th Parachute Infantry Unit Journal, 13 September–16 October 1944.

505th Parachute Infantry A/A Report 'Invasion of Holland', 17 September–16 October 1944.

505th Parachute Infantry 'S-3 Journal Bigot Market', 17 September–18 October 1944.

506th Parachute Infantry Unit Journal, 14 September–22 October 1944.

British Army records

1st Airborne Division Report on Operation 'MARKET' Arnhem, 17–28 Sep 1944 (copy RG 407).

1st Airborne Division Headquarters war diary, September 1944 (www.pegasusarchive.org).

2nd and 3rd Battalions Irish Guards war diaries, September 1944, National Archives UK (courtesy of Mark Hickman).

Primary Sources

Ambrose, S., *Band of Brothers. E Company, 506th Regiment, 101st Airborne from Normandy to Hitler's Eagle's Nest*, Simon and Schuster, New York, 1992.

Bennett, R., *Ultra in the West. The Normandy Campaign of 1944–45*, Charles Scribner's Sons, New York, 1979.

Blumenson, M., *Breakout and Pursuit*, Office of the Chief of Military History, Washington DC, 1969.

Bradley, O., *A Soldier's Story*, Henry Holt and Company, New York, 1951.

Cole, H., *The Lorraine Campaign*, Office of the Chief of Military History, Washington DC, 1950.

Collins, L. and Lapierre, D., *Is Paris Burning?*, Simon and Schuster, New York, 1965.

de Guingan, F., *Operation Victory*, Charles Scribner's Sons, New York, 1947.

Eisenhower, D., *Crusade in Europe*, Doubleday & Company, Garden City, 1948.

Ellis, L.F. with Warhurst, A.E., *Victory in the West Volume II The Defeat of Germany*, HMSO, London, 1968.

FitzGerald, D.J.L., *History of the Irish Guards in the Second World War*, Gale & Polden, Aldershot, 1949.

Florentin, E., *The Battle of the Falaise Gap*, Elck Books, London, 1965, original title *Stalingrad en Normandie*, Presses de la Cité, Paris, 1964.

Fussell, P., *The Boys' Crusade. The American Infantry in Northwestern Europe, 1944–1945*, The Modern Library/Random House, New York, 2003.

Gavin, J., diary January 1944–September 1945, United States Army Military History Institute, Carlisle.

Gavin, J., *On to Berlin. Battles of an Airborne Commander 1943–1946*, The Viking Press, New York, 1978.

Hastings, M., *Overlord: D-Day and the Battle for Normandy*, Simon and Schuster, New York, 1984.

Hemingway, E., 'A Room on the Garden Side', *Strand Magazine*, June–October 2018, pp. 6, 8 and 10.

Horrocks, B. with Belfield, E. and Essame, H., *Corps Commander*, Charles Scribner's Sons, New York, 1977.

Keegan, J., *Six Armies in Normandy: From D-Day to the Liberation of Paris*, Jonathan Cape Ltd, 1982, reprinted by Penguin Books Ltd, Harmonsworth, 1984.

Kennett, L., *G.I.: The American Soldier in World War II*, Charles Scribner's Sons, New York, 1987.

Liddell Hart, B., *History of the Second World War*, Putnam's Sons, New York, 1971.

MacDonald, C., 'River Crossing at Arnaville' in *Three Battles: Arnaville, Altuzzo and Schmidt* by MacDonald, C. and Mathews, S., pp. 1–99, Office of the Chief of Military History, Washington DC, 1952.

MacDonald, C., 'Objective: Schmidt' in *Three Battles: Arnaville, Altuzzo and Schmidt* by MacDonald, C. and Mathews, S., pp. 251–422, Office of the Chief of Military History, Washington DC, 1952.

MacDonald, C., *The Siegfried Line Campaign*, Office of the Chief of Military History, Washington DC, 1963.

Marshall, S.L.A. and Westover, J., Battalion and Small Unit Studies 1944–45, National Archives RG 407: (No. 1) 1st Battalion, 501st Parachute Infantry, Holland; (No. 6) 502nd Parachute Infantry at Best, Holland 17–19 September 1944; (draft) 502–1 at St Oedenrode.

Mauldin, B., *Up Front*, Henry Holt and Company, New York, 1945.

Meyer, H., *History of the 12th SS Panzer Division Hitlerjugend* Volume II, J.J. Fedorwicz Publishing, Winnipeg, 1994, translated by H. Henshler; reprinted by Stackpole Books, Harrisburg, 2005.

Montgomery, B., *The Memoirs of Field-Marshal the Viscount Montgomery of Alamein, KG*, World Publishing Company, Cleveland, 1958.

Patton, G., *War As I Knew It*, Houghton Mifflin Company, New York, 1947, reprinted by Bantam Books, New York, 1979.

Richardson, E.R. and Allan, S., *Quartermaster Supply in the European Theatre of Operations in World War II, Vol. II Subsistence*, The Quartermaster School, Camp Lee, Virginia, 1948.

Richardson, E.R. and Allan, S., *Quartermaster Supply in the European Theatre of Operations in World War II, Vol. III Outfitting the Soldier*, The Quartermaster School, Camp Lee, Virginia, 1948.

Ryan, C., *A Bridge Too Far*, Simon & Schuster, New York, 1974.

Thuring, G. and Heij, J., *Verdwenen Kerkhoven Molenhoek – Nebo – Sophiaweg Nijmegen Area – Holland. Vanished (Temp) Cemeteries*, Bevrijdingsmuseum 1944, Groesbeek, 1989.

Urquhart, R.E. with Greatorex, W., *Arnhem*, Cassell & Company Ltd, 1958, reprinted by Pen & Sword Military, Barnsley, 2007.

Wilmot, C., *The Struggle for Europe*, Harper and Brothers, New York, 1952.

Notes

Notes

Notes

Larry's Cold Cuts
939-0110